YOU DON'T HAVE TO LIVE SAD TO BE HUMAN:

Harvest the Positive Power in You

SELDA SALMON

Order this book online at www.trafford.com/07-1152
or email orders@trafford.com

Most Trafford titles are also available at major online book retailers.

Note for Librarians: A cataloguing record for this book is available from Library and Archives Canada at www.collectionscanada.ca/amicus/index-e.html

ISBN: 978-1-4251-3139-5

We at Trafford believe that it is the responsibility of us all, as both individuals and corporations, to make choices that are environmentally and socially sound. You, in turn, are supporting this responsible conduct each time you purchase a Trafford book, or make use of our publishing services. To find out how you are helping, please visit www.trafford.com/responsiblepublishing.html

Our mission is to efficiently provide the world's finest, most comprehensive book publishing service, enabling every author to experience success. To find out how to publish your book, your way, and have it available worldwide, visit us online at www.trafford.com/10510

www.trafford.com

North America & international
toll-free: 1 888 232 4444 (USA & Canada)
phone: 250 383 6864 ♦ fax: 250 383 6804 ♦ email: info@trafford.com

The United Kingdom & Europe
phone: +44 (0)1865 722 113 ♦ local rate: 0845 230 9601
facsimile: +44 (0)1865 722 868 ♦ email: info.uk@trafford.com

10 9 8 7 6 5 4 3 2

FOREWORD

GREAT teachers strive to educate richly their students of all ages. They are what I describe as ideal books, simply because their hearts are always so open to giving knowledge to the willing minds that hope for the greatness that brings about positive changes.

The various ways in which I present this book includes simple ideas that I am hopeful will make a big positive contribution to your life. It is with the joy of a new peaceful awareness, enormous enthusiasm and sincerity that I pray you will find this book comforting, encouraging, and insightful as you draw great strength from it. From this day forward may you desire even more positive emotional and spiritual growth.

CONTRIBUTIONS

"I GIVE pleasure, not pain" is for me unforgettable words said to me and fellow classmates years ago by a somewhat misunderstood professor who made it quite clear moments after saying them. They are words meant to be used for success, not for failure. He then went on to talk about the power of humanity's contributions. I found this very interesting because "Contribution" as you know can bring great pain or great joy. It depends on what we ourselves contribute or what is contributed to us. What we contribute to our fellow human beings and to this planet of ours as we journey through our limited days really does matter. How we affect the lives of others, good or bad, doesn't always end with the downing of one sunset.

I speak to you not only as a human being who lives conscious of the true meaning of contribution, but as a fellow human being whose own formative years were extremely painful, due to the selfishness and thoughtlessness of others. Even more unfortunately for me, the emotional pain did not end in my childhood. The memories haunted me into too many of my adult years. The good news is I no longer live in the pain and fear of the past. I refuse to allow painful contributions—past or present—to keep me from being the whole person I was created to be. At the same time, it's only fair I tell you, I did not arrive at this place of peace with the past overnight. It was a long, painful journey done in the raw—no cushion of any kind.

The day I decided to stop believing I was born to suffer is the day I also decided what it would be like to live without the intense hidden emotional pain that was so much a part of who I was. My emotional pain was kept so well hidden it and I had become one in the same, so much so it was manifesting itself in areas of my life that was best left without such harsh realities. I went to sleep in emotional pain. I woke up in emotional pain. And each time these fires began to burn, it would burn deeper.

In spite of the fact that I was created in perfect balance, I needed a good effort. On more than one occasion, sadness demanded to take over my life completely. It wanted to become the permanent boss of me. It was then that I realized I was going to have to fight for renewal. I was going to have to start shoveling. I was going to have to dig out those memories and deal with them in a way I had feared my whole life up to then. Lucky for me, that decision came in the nick of time. Had I continued to deny the realities of an extremely painful childhood, that denial might have destroyed me. By burying the past as deeply as it was in my very soul, I left it to take root—roots that were growing deeper into my mind.

As I began to heal, I found out to my amazement that during those years of sadness, my life was a shade of gray I had grown accustomed to. It's very difficult to enjoy any area of your life when you are rooted in pain. When we have to bury an emotional problem rather than dealing with it, we are saying that this is beyond me. It is way more than I am capable of dealing with. It's just too much for me, and sometimes it really is. Preserving one's own sanity has to be number one priority. But I can tell you from my own experience as a fellow human being, dealing with emotional pain instead of leaving it to sour even more is a better way to survive. Anything that erodes the human spirit must be removed fast. Every eroded treasure deserves restoration. You are the most precious of all treasures. Those painful contributions that were forced upon us, when we bury them for so long that they begin to take root, you can bet your life, sooner or later, they will branch out on us as well and keep us from having the most productive life possible. It must be dealt with. If for you that means dealing with your kind of emotional pain one tiny piece at a time, then so be it!

Not everyone can find the strength needed straight away to dig up and remove every piece all at once. It has to be a slow process. One step at a time is the only way, but I guarantee you on my own survival, you will become an emotionally stronger human being each time you are able to overcome an offending piece. The buried childhood memories that were too painful to face in my early adult years are the reason that without intending to, I also buried a part of myself. I was—in a bizarre way—comfortable in the misery of how I accepted my life. I had become an agent of pain extension. As a result, I saw myself as having less value. As horrible as that sounds, that's how it was with my soul.

All was far from well. I was allowing a painful past to picture the future. I had days when all of the worst memories would flood my mind in competition for intensity. I recalled them with painful detailed accuracies it was getting progressively worse. There was a full scale war in my being. I should have been celebrating my life instead.

You should also know that I was not always conscious of the power the past had on my life. I did not realize how it influenced the most important decisions in my life. For me, the realization of what I needed to do about my life, the step I needed to take towards healing was itself almost as painful as the wicked contributions made to my formative years. I had no idea how to go about giving up my front row seat in the building of deeply rooted quiet anger that I often used to inflict even more emotional pain on myself.

During the years of healing tears, my most painful realization was this. If I were to survive to experience life as it was intended for all humans to, I would have to stop running to denial. I would have to stop telling myself that it's okay to go on as I was. It was too emotionally tiring. I needed to turn around, face the realities of my childhood horrors and become the stronger root in order to branch out in the right ways. And I needed to do so fast.

I desperately needed a healthier way of living. I was lost in emotional anguish for far too long. The unpleasant alterations to my life I kept experiencing had to end. I needed to branch out in ways that would make any abuser envious. I had to stop allowing the past to invade my God-given right to a peaceful existence. I could not continue to give the past so much power over me. There needed to be a better way of managing my life directly.

The loss of inner peace was alarming. The lack of natural beauty had my life upside down. The full impact of sadness moved my life from the safer places God intended. The constant deeply hidden sadness was forcing me to live in a miniature life. The silent hidden-at-the-bottom-of-the-well war against myself was sucking the life out of me. I was not only wasting energy, I was also wasting days, wasting my precious life. My life should have been a lovely one. Instead, I became a magnet for pain.

I had to find a way to defeat the memories before I became too weak to. I needed to render those memories powerless. And in order to do so, I needed to harvest the positive power in me. My God-given power was not being put to good use. I had to come to the realization that I could not allow such horrible memories to keep robbing me of the future. I got to the point in my life when I could no longer afford the deepening effects that were threatening to wipe out my life. My primary source of peace needed for regeneration was not being harvested. One of the most important questions I had to ask myself was, "How can anyone who keeps reliving a painful past and using those toxic remembrances to assault their soul ever find peace?"

I would never suggest to anyone who has been abused that they forget the past or pretend their life was not treated with carelessness and cruelty. I am suggesting those memories, however cruel, be used to one's own advantage. This will, without question, make you the wiser. This is not an action of success you need to fear. Hanging on to plaguing issues is very damaging to your mind, body, and soul. Waking up each day bracing yourself for more abnormalities is just scarring injuries no innocent soul can afford.

I can tell you from first hand experience, it is not always good to allow the past to take the lead into your future. Only the most positive energies should determine the future. No matter how desperate your situation in life might be, there is always at your disposal faith that you are free to use to bring hope. If you must keep experiences from your past permanently rooted in your life, don't let it be the painful experiences you have suffered. You are the best treasure that there is. Treat yourself as such.

Too many of us treasures who were abused in our most delicate formative years have yet to be discovered by self. Some victims of abuse are still lacking their truest sense of self. Removing the painful remembrances from the controls was not easy. It was too worthwhile to be. It took my best efforts. If as you read this you are saying to yourself, "I wouldn't know where to begin the healing process; my wounds are too deep," then why not start by making yourself a love project. Love yourself enough to take all the steps necessary for healing. Get a new perspective. The longer you continue to live in sadness, the more of yourself will be lost. Give yourself the gift that is as precious as you are. Give yourself the gift of love. You will enjoy more of life's beautiful things.

Discover a whole new world of peace. Be as vibrant and free in your spirit as when you first left heaven. A whole new you will not be something you have to imagine. A whole new you cannot only be visible to you starting now. A whole new you can be a divine reality. As you tune into your own life, you can advance much more than you ever thought possible.

Always keep in mind that whatever you imagine for yourself can be manifested in reality. Imagine your life in a permanent forward mode. When I decided it was time to take my mind back from sadness in order to live freedom, I also decided to make myself the most important, the most precious, and the most valuable project I had ever worked on in my entire life. I am a love project that I am still working on to date—and will be for the rest of my life as I live with a sense of urgency.

Obviously, life does have its price, but for those of us who were abused as children, physically, or emotionally, that price is way too high, especially when those painful memories are given the power to control the rest of our lives. Reinforcing yourself as the most important authority in you life here on earth is a must for survival. The same holds true for able body adults in present abusive situations. There is a much better way to live. There is nothing positive to gain from allowing yourself to be abused. How much unfair suffering does anyone need to endure before realizing you are dumping the only precious life that you have? Allowing past or present abusive situations to control your life is a disastrous journey that could produce lethal results. If you are presently in an abusive relationship, eliminate it before it eliminates you. There is no question that the experience of childhood abuse can lead to poor choices in adulthood. But before you start beating up on yourself with regrets, keep in mind that nothing prepares a child for abuse. The poor choices made in adulthood as a result should not be used as an excuse for self hatred. Our lives were not meant to be locked in a permanent embrace of misery. No life was meant to be a journey of disasters.

There was a time in my life when on a subconscious level I had this sense of duty to pain. Without realizing it, I became a willing sponge, always ready to soak up as much pain as my mind could hold. I never went a full week without recalling some horror scene from my childhood days—always unplanned. I never knew when, where, or what would trigger a memory. I was always caught off guard and removed from the moment without my resistance. Without realizing it, I was giving those toxic memories permission to slice up my life. I would relive every horror filled moment in vivid colors.

Once I was back there in yester year, reliving those hellish memories, I would try in as many ways as my weary mind would allow to reverse the most brutal of events. Needless to say, this ritualistically easy-to-start emotional pain was very costly. Recalling these cruel memories was limiting my life. I was inflicting the same pain on myself over and over again. I knew there had to be an ending somehow, but I was alone with my inner anger and anguish, so I thought. I needed an intelligent embrace. The pain in my mind and soul was as real as it gets. The human predators were still walking powerfully in my mind. They were still assaulting me. They were still way over the lines that were crossed.

The horrible evil acts against my humanity were still laying claim to my life. These memories no one else could see was horrifically haunting. The human mind as you know can carry quietly the evidence of past horrors that hide themselves from the eyes of strangers, family and friends. My mind was too often still bearing witness to the barbaric inhumanities of a child's worst nightmares. My own mind was not a safe place to be. I could find no refuge in it. I found only the memories that were hell bent on being first as they recreated the worst of emotional pain. This placed my focus much more on the past than it was on the present. In my recollections, I was no doubt making myself even more vulnerable to the kinds of destruction that come with quiet anguish. I was without a doubt condemning myself to a life of emotional pain. I was living my life directed by wrong reasons. Being wronged by fellow human beings who did not possess an ounce of self respect or human decency should never be used as a guideline for your life. I spent years…let me rephrase that. I wasted years of my life walking every breath through someone else's evil rules.

Bad remembrances were controlling me, and I had no idea how to demand joy for myself. It was like living with a fever I had no idea how to get rid of. I knew I was not happy the way I see some people being, but the kind of alertness that I should have had just wasn't there. Evil legacy had me bogged down. I was a living breathing human industry of emotional pain. I could not afford to be, but I was. At one point in my life, I was so busy filling up my mind with these toxic remembrances that only God Himself could find room in there for improvement. What a powerfully positive difference it would have made if I realized back then what is my better reality today. Had I not been taught at an early age how to be a pain sponge, I would not have allowed myself to be taken away so often and be used by the most wicked of memories. I would never have allowed so many visits. I was still being preyed upon by past evil deeds, a severe punishment I did nothing to deserve.

As I grew into adulthood, I tried on more than one occasion to muster the strength and courage needed to break the bondage but thought the roots of pain was anchored too deeply to be removed. I found it easier to give those roots the opportunity they needed to grow even deeper into my soul. That kind of acceptance running through the center of my life offered no protection whatsoever. The divine ties were being torn apart. The deep wounds and the emotional pain that resulted were slowly, but surely pulling me further and further away from my true destiny. I was not in a protected area, divinely speaking.

I needed to put my life back into the peaceful environment the creator of the universe gifted me with long before I was even placed into my mother's womb. I needed those well thought out benefits in the safer place that had always been mine for the taking. Instead, I became a popular attraction for pain. This was not the right increase I needed for emotional wellness. This constant old growth was allowed to be more serious than I was. It had a technique that developed with my permission and loomed larger with each unpleasant change. These looming shadows kept pulling me into a well of toxic memories. The terrifying aftershocks were still happening, still quietly wounding me even thought I was not responsible for the original crimes against my humanity. I was only responsible for giving them the power to stick around years after the grim facts.

I was still allowing myself to be assaulted with brute force, still being robbed of the greatest of human freedom. The touches of past evils were still barging into my mind at the most inconvenient of times, making it far more difficult to secure joy. The intensity of these painful remembrances was ordering me out of my own life. It was the kinds of emotional pain that dries the human bones. The calculated wickedness that came to bear on my most innocent of years was still bearing down on my life like a heavy flood of pollution. I was drowning in violent memories and had no idea how to keep these nightmares from accessing my life. I had more experience in fear than in fighting. There was a growing demand from these most violent of memories for all of me.

I need you to understand how the very best of your humanity can be stolen right before your very eyes. You may not realize how easily until your remaining breaths can be counted on one hand. Without past abusers in my immediate environment, I was still being robbed. I was allowing the remembrances to rob from my life. The definition of predator could not only be found in my abusers but could also be found in every mirror that I could see myself in. As the shadows loomed, I was becoming, at least in my mind, a tiny speck of humanity.

One prefers not to remember, yet with every painful remembrance starting from scratch, the pressure continued to mount. My standing up to the emotional pain was far from grand. I was too often the heap in the corner of the room wondering how life can be this cruel. I was so sad I hated being human. I desperately needed help and still had no idea how to help myself out of the valley of evil shadows that haunted me.

There were few and far in between days when I would demand a change from myself. I have to take better care of my mind, I would reason, a determination that lasted only as long as the arrival of the old memories that were even more determined to convince me they had me reduced. Prolonged sadness is a tough position for anyone to be in. It's a massive block, but not one that is impossible to remove. In spite of the abuse I suffered in my childhood, I could never have imagined myself growing up to become a pain collector, but that's what resulted. That's what I became, not consciously of course, yet pain became a very big part of my life as a result of trusting the wrong people. You would think that someone like myself who experienced such an emotionally and physically painful childhood would have grown up very mistrusting of my fellow human beings. Instead, in my desperation to be loved, appreciated, and comforted, I gravitated to those who had none of the above to offer me. I had to learn through difficulties that resulted from my bad choices that I have the same value as any other human being with the right to demand my trust be earned.

Having said that, I think it is only fair that I add the following reminder. We can, as you know, trust another human being with our soul for as long as fifty years or more only to discover suddenly and violently our trust had been misplaced. Can't we? This reminder is not meant to frighten, only to make a point. Too many of us who grew up in an anguish-filled environment is left with emotional needs we seek to fulfill in adulthood, a neediness that is sometimes taken advantage of by others who themselves have no idea how to love. Too many times in my desire to find inner peace by way of human friendship, I discovered my trust was horribly misplaced.

After years of calling the wrong people "friend," emotional pain became a signature I wore as I would a favorite piece of garment. I allowed these bad choices to waste precious fast moving days. The realization that I had, on a subconscious level, pronounced myself a failure had yet to be. I was still interrogating myself in spite of the fact that no child can think like an adult. For the simple fact, no child is wise in the ways of the world, therefore thinks like a child, acts like a child. I was like so many an innocent child when the worst of man's inhumanity to man took place in my life. I did nothing to deserve crucifixion, yet there I was as an adult more than a little willing to sacrifice the rest of my days to the past and the madness of toxic evil selfish souls. I was allowing the bitter memories to be the driving force in my life. It was slowly cutting a path of destruction through my life. As a result, I gave up my ability to see myself in any of the lovingly rich ways that the creator of my life sees me. The cruel disappointments the damage and destruction still imprinted on my mind kept me from recognizing or acknowledging all of the Divine's positive power that was mine to use. I was in a contributing role I should not have been. The things I desperately needed to contribute to my life were also the opportunities I needed for freedom. I was not as aware then as I am now that no one can bring back a single hour. I failed to face the fact that it is not only leaves that can be lost to the wind. I was still very much a victim denied justice in a prison of sadness I had invited to stay years longer than it should have. Clearly, I needed to protect myself against the memories of abuse that made me feel reduced. Trying to patch up the areas of my life that were still eroding was not going to be good enough. Reducing the risk of insanity was not going to be good enough. Neither would pretending all is well be good enough. I needed to eliminate all together the belief that in order to be human I had to accept daily sadness as a part of my humanity, in spite of the fact that God was remarkably accurate when He created me. Instead of accepting myself as one of the beautiful varieties, I saw myself as having less value. In that kind of negative acceptance, there was no room for a healthy self image. Like billions of people in the world today, there was no one in my childhood environment who truly understood how to value their own humanity because they were not taught how to. It continues still, too many innocent children around the world are still being denied the opportunity to grow up in the peaceful environment that would teach them the true value of their humanity. I have met people who suffered similar types of abuse in their childhood as I did, who now as adults will tell you in the most violently angry offensive tone while standing in the middle of the obvious circle of destruction that they were taught to create for themselves, that they are one hundred percent certain that the abuse they suffered as a child had no lasting effect on their lives, that they were able to escape unscathed. Not true! No one, no matter who you are, male or female, rich or poor, escapes abuse, whether physical or emotional, unscathed. Abuse of any kind always has an effect. We are, after all, human beings with the God-given right to live a peaceful comfortable life. Everyone knows that in an abusive situation things are not equal or fair. There are so many excuses for abuse as there are people on our planet, which means we will never be able to make sense of the wrong doings. I don't know any child who enjoys being abused. Who really knows why some of our fellow human beings prefer to contribute evil? In spite of the fact that I was so badly abused as a child, I cannot imagine abusing another innocent human being. The thousands of times that I re-traumatized myself with toxic remembrances was not in any way intentional. I did not realize at the time how much I was abusing myself. Like those other victims of abuse lost in mental anguish, I too did not realize how heavy the pile of garbage forced on my formative years would become. The heaviest reality came calling years ago on a very hot summer day while traveling by train from Baltimore, Maryland to New York. I had a flashback, a horrible memory brought back by the innocent comment of another passenger. In those horror filled days, my emotional pain was so deeply rooted and well organized that all those memories needed was the first moment of my attention to conduct themselves into a hellish symphony of remembrances. Retrieving myself from its embrace was not even a thought. I did not feel big enough or powerful enough to reject the unfair sentence that had been placed on my life. Negative energy had a closer relationship with my heart than I did. I am blessed to have a heart that refused to let me fall down, even though I knew it was not existing in the right reality. The pain that I allowed to track me for most of my life up until then became a full fiery traveling companion that day. Its sick seduction stole my attention and held it so long and so undivided that before I realized it, I had spent the entire train ride revisiting the past, giving more power to my abusers and allowing the memories to help me figure out clever ways to hide my tears from the rest of the passengers who could see me. I was so weighed down with the guilt and shame that belonged on the heads and in the hearts of my abusers. That garbage did not belong to me. I had no business carrying it as though it were a prized piece of luggage. Unfortunately, I allowed a few more years of horror filled flashbacks to control me. During that time, it's fair to say there were at least a full fifteen percent yearly pain increase in my soul. I was still giving my mind permission to pick up where my despicable repugnant abusers had left off, a dangerous allowance no decent mind needs. During this time, I truly had no idea how desperate I was for even a brief recess. Once I began the journey back from the edge, I found that I had also begun to give myself the kinds of human freedom I once thought too luxurious for me to indulge in, such as sleeping in late on a Sunday morning. It was on one of these beautiful occasions that I asked myself, what if I were standing in the middle of the most beautiful deliciously smelling lavender garden on earth and someone walked up to me with what is obviously a very heavy, full bag of garbage that had the most awful, offensive odors and ordered me to hold it for them as close to my body as possible, and keep standing there with it for the rest of the day? What would I say to them? I am sure I would have a few ideas of the places they could put their garbage instead. So why then, I wondered, was I still holding onto the garbage forces on my life when I was too young to decide for myself? For any adult to continue carrying such toxic essences is to remain a helpless, powerless child. Every civilized, sane, decent, human being all over the world knows that the selfishness of some of our fellow human beings in authority often leads to the abuse of freewill. Human ignorance is rarely ever harmless either. Don't force yourself to continue holding onto garbage that is not yours to keep. Abuse of the innocent is among the worst of human garbage behavior. This does not belong in your life. Drop it and run to the cover that the Divine's provided for you. Don't take on the responsibilities of your abuser or abusers. They are the ones who should feel shame, fear and guilt. The reason for any child's existence is not to carry garbage from toxic adults into their own adulthood. You are not responsible for the living hell that was forced on your life. The violators of innocence don't lose sleep over their evil deeds. You are not ruling their lives by being sad. Don't let them rule yours. Let your enemy or enemies know that like your body, your mind is also yours alone. Don't let any one or anything evil live in your mind. Evil doers prey upon the weak. Most victims of abuse are vulnerable, unable to defend themselves, as you know. You are no longer a helpless child.

With this in mind, it is wise not to risk ruining the rest of your life because of a terrible experience. Your life should not be what gets arrested. However long the abuse you suffered went on – a minute or two – was way more than long enough. Don't add anymore suffering time. You have suffered long enough. Advance, don't revert. Don't keep getting stung. Evil should not be allowed to steal your true voice or your life. Your most important life's decisions should not reflect inner turmoil. Dealing with the memories of abuse is never easy, especially if you are one of those people who were abused by the selfish, thoughtless, cruel hypocrites who were responsible for your safety and comfort. You should not be helping your abuser to continue the cycle of abuse by molesting your mind with these upsets. We know that there is no vaccine against these painful remembrances. It will take your own inner powers to survive better. It is not safe to continue suffering. No one ever finds life saving substances in this kind of powerless obsession. If stress is allowed to continue deciding for you the most crushing of mind inhabitations will most certainly take from you your most precious abundance. As long as you are alive, these memories may never go away, but they do not have to continue to control you. These memories do not have to determine your future. Having a great life must be first, regardless of the past that you cannot change. The realities you find most awful does not have to keep dragging you down. It's the wrong focus. Don't let the tragic consequences of being abused continue to include you. Living one's life controlled by past or present abuse is too great a sacrifice for anyone to make. You have the positive power needed to make a radical departure from the destructive memories. There is a major restoring force in you, the likes of which you have never seen. There is so much positive power in you yet to be experience. You can be set free. You were not born a lamb for slaughter. Mental anguish does not have to engulf and defeat your confidence. Reverse your thinking. Start giving your life the special gentle attention it deserves. Choose today to be a survivor. Start reconstructing your mind the right way. I guarantee you will find and start enjoying your truest self. All things are possible if you only believe. You can reconstruct a more fulfilling life. You don't have to get to your last breath still waiting to start living a better life. There are emotions so destructive they lack any hope at all. The decision to live free of constant emotional pain is a decision you are free to make. When you do, you will discover the greatness of your life. Living your best life should not be delayed. It should be done while you still have the opportunity to breathe. No one who has ever suffered any kind of abuse has ever been left in the best of shape. In spite of this reality, you can still give yourself the gift of a second chance to be as beautifully bold as you were meant to be. You are priceless, my dear, not powerless. There is a far better reality for you to live with. It is a reality that will not only spread hope throughout your entire life. Included will be deserving miracles. No matter how badly you feel, it does not have to destroy your life. With your permission, the long suffering can end. You are a lot more powerful than the gatherings. Those despicable reruns that keep injuring you are preventable. These cruel surprises from the past that are given your permission to keep advancing can be rendered powerless. It is unfair that to date in this so-called modern world in which we reside, some abusers of the innocent still get to live a better life than their victims. This reality in itself can create some uneasiness for the abused. Your life can still soar, in spite of it. No one should be given the power to continue breaking down your life. You are not the person that you should be condemning. Let the reminder that you were not created for any type of abuse, become one of the guidance for your life. You were born to live the highest quality of life possible. Turn this fact into a reward for your pain and sufferings. You can leave the past a free person, as free as you were born to be. Turn the darkest days of your life into the brightest future any human being can have. You are the greatest of ideas developed and brought to breath. Live like it. You are very significant. It is why you were assigned heavenly angels. Don't be intimidated by the past. Withdraw your life from tragedy. You can break the bond. Stop allowing past or present abuse to keep you from enjoying the God given freedom of your life. You were not given life so you can suffer at the hands of fellow human beings. It is not a storage shed for garbage. The courage and strength you were not able to harvest as a child is yours to use now. Aside from your Creator, you are your best life insurance here on earth. Take the very best care of you. Keep yourself happy. It is so easy to convince yourself you don't fit into life because of all that you have suffered. Well, you can feel secure in the fact that you are not an imitation human. Therefore, you do fit in. You are a huge positive difference that needs to love you more. Love makes good efforts easier, especially in difficult times. Instead of continuing to be an emotional pain institution, choose to be your best earthly support, and anticipate only the most joyful things. If you really want to experience your best life, refuse discouraging thoughts. In spite of cruel adversities, the miracle of you should never be taken for granted. You should never become common to you. There is nothing common about the divine Power that created you. It is foolish to see yourself as anything less than the greatest of creations. Your hands were not created to reach for defeat. You have what it takes to renew and reshape your spirit at your disposal. Any life under the weight of sadness is a life being kept from its true purpose. You are so valuable to the Creator that special blessings were created just for you, but it is not easy to deliver blessings to someone who is buried deeply beneath emotional pain. It is a living death. Certain blessings were not created for the dead. In order to receive your blessings, you must get out from under and reclaim your rightful place in life while you still have breath. Start receiving and enjoying. You are missing your best blessings. Sadness that results from abuse of any kind is rapidly blighting. You know by now I speak from experience. Depression is a paralyzing grounding emotion. It ruins many lives before the realization of a price too high. The days that we are blessed to remain earth bound should be spent doing good things that are as great as we were created to be. The gift of life should pay off in a big way for everyone. Injuries and suffering as you already know is not a part of the Divine's plan. Life should always include a variety of joyful experiences. We are designed for happiness. It is sinful for you yourself to make contributions for a lesser life. It is possible for you to face the nightmares of the past and wake up to a winner's life. The damage was done. We cannot change the past realities, but we can create better ones. You can secure the joy that is meant for your life. You do not have to live with a broken heart until the end of days. There are many important steps that you can take that will enable you to move forward and start demanding the best from life. Neglecting your happiness is an extreme you don't need. No human beings should have to live their life with a feeling of worthlessness because of crimes committed against their humanity. You did not invite betrayal. The sinful acts against you should not be used as an excuse to devalue you. Where is the justice in that? You are not the enemy. Don't surrender your life to that which is. You can return to the life you were meant to have. You are in possession of an incredible amount of positive power that can aid in the removal of lethal toxic reactions. Living your life with hidden mental anguish will continue to leave you feeling as though you are being hunted, almost too tired to stay alive. You are not a fantasy. You are a reality. It is a mistake to live your entire life fantasizing about the happiness you wish you had. If the only thing standing between yourself and happiness is your sadness, it's time you take back your life. It's time for you to flourish. When sadness takes control, it numbs and weakens you. That is not a good way to live. You are a living, breathing human being with remarkable built-in potential. Don't waste it! You are too precious. Time is too short for us humans. We don't get enough of it. We can not afford to spare any of it for anything that does not provide the right kinds of substance. You were created from all things good. You are the best of the best, which is why when anything less is applied to your life, it does not feel good to you. Remove yourself from violence, past or present. Show respect, love and appreciation for the Divine power that brought you into being. You are the result of the most advanced Power. Clear your mind of the lingering garbage, and become a force to be reckoned with. Most abusers are cowards. Don't let them make one out of you. Show evil that you are far more powerful. Use the divine power that you were created from. Power is what brought you. You don't have to spend the rest of your life struggling for control of your own life. That is not how your precious gift of life should be spent. Don't live on the short leash that the lovers of evil put you on. Don't withdraw your life from its powerful place because someone else convinced you they had the power to leave you an empty shell. You are not an empty vessel. You are full of all of the power you need to survive and improve your life. You are the evidence of the greatest power, don't you know? Offer yourself the opportunity to use it. You have that resource. Don't hide from it. Don't let anyone convince you that you have to stay down at the place you were knocked down for the rest of your life. Get up, face the forces of evil, and show them who is BOSS. A moment of clarity should be every moment that you are awake. Come up for air and use the positive power reinforcement in you.

You don't lack the guts. You contain more power than you can live long enough to use up. You don't need to accept into your humanity the feelings of insecurities. Some deviant slapped on you. You are nobody's fool. Don't keep those wounds bleeding the way I did. Recognize the beauty of you, and stop neglecting your life. That's what prolonged sadness does. It causes people to neglect themselves, to neglect their most important needs. It's like being exiled with barely enough to survive. The something missing from your life should not be your attention. Your commitment should not be to a mental institution. Your commitment should be to loving yourself. There are so many wonderful things in life to explore. Why give up your best life opportunities so that sadness can wreck your life. Despite the fact you have suffered so much, you can re-energize your life. While you still have breath, any kind of breakdown in communication should not be with yourself. Offer yourself the most peaceful devotion that you can. You and I both know that there are more than a few people willing to use the life of a child in the most evil ways, but unlike too many of the innocent little victims of abuse, you can survive. The fact that you are still alive is proof of that. You made it this far, didn't you? You have the inner strength to muster. With courage that will bring you liberation, your life can be transformed. Endless blessings can be yours. Have no doubt about that. You were created with dignity. The corrupt should not influence or take from any area of your life. The ultimate power does not belong to abusive deviants. The finest of examples has never been set by the worst among us. Remain faithful to the beauty and preciousness of your humanity. Rejoice in the dawning of each new day, despite past insults and other abuses. You can accomplish powerful things. The first and most important opportunity that you need is still in every breath that you take. You are the greatest most valuable thing that you own. There is nothing that is equal in value to the human soul. You have in your possession a perfect human life not to be wasted. Wasting even a single day in sadness is an enormous loss. I know how harsh that sounds, but it's true. We are all guilty of it, even though no one's sadness has every bought anyone back from the dead. The painful blighting sacrifice of depression has never solved the problems of mankind. It only adds to the problems we have already created for ourselves, problems we have too much of on our planet. It is not necessary for you to suffer indefinitely. Impaling yourself on grief is such a waste of precious life. The peace of mind that you need for more self-respect is only a heart beat away. Have faith that you can prevail. This kind of attitude will contribute to your happiness. If you are not the abuser, you should not be living with a guilty conscience. Neither should you be living with feelings of hopelessness. Your clean conscience should give you peace of mind. You do not belong to sorrow. You have the courage you need to withdraw your life from its grip. Because someone else with an untidy life and major filthy behavior was careless with your soul does not mean you have to be careless with it as well. Tomorrow can be a lot better than today. The decision to accept the peaceful life you were meant to have is a decision that should not be an impossible one to make. With your permission, love and devotion, your journey of success can begin. Great can be your faithfulness. Trust that you do not have to spend the rest of your days with an aching heart. You can find love, comfort, peace and joy. You can still live an amazing life, in spite of past disappointments. Speak your needs, faith it, and the Divine's love will bring it to pass, providing your prayers are for positive good things. Are you one of those people who have gone what might be thought of as half the length of your life (although now days that's anybody's guess, since we are living so much longer) and are only now realizing how much your life has been held back because of abuse? It's not too late to make a positive contribution to your own life. There is still a lot of youth left in you. Please don't continue giving permission to negative influences. You don't need that. The awful pain of abuse is very disruptive. It keeps you away from your best life. It does not have to continue to be so. As a fellow human being, I do realize that in spite of our best efforts, sadness is certainly one of the most human of emotions. But the fact remains, you do not have to live in sadness in order to be human. I believe that after we survive from infancy to adulthood, what we do with the gift of life, we were given is entirely up to us. This is especially true for those of us living in a free society. Some people prefer to pretend to be happy when they can actually make happiness a true reality. Why not reclaim your life before your days are done. Invite the winds of positive changes. This will allow you to be an inspiration to others. The same power that taught the birds to sing is waiting for your willingness to embrace your life fully. This very day can be the beginning of a new chapter in your life. You should not be feeling shame or embarrassment because of the evil applies to your life that you did not invite. Life should be rewarding, but not in an evil way. It is not difficult to understand why peace for the human soul is so important. It is only through the Divine's intent can we find hope and great joy. Sadness is a very bad course for any one to pursue, a badness that can damage the mind. You have it within your power to end this bad force forever. You can live a life so beautiful you will be envied. The spiritual growth needed for strength and permanent positive change is yours to begin. In spite of these troubled times that we are living in, Jehovah is still powerful. Those of us who respect and appreciate the power and love used to create a single life knows that the innocent should never suffer, we can see the horrible injustices in the behaviors of some of our fellow human beings that can sometimes leave us feeling that life is just not worth living. Yet in spite of all the horror-filled disappointments, great and wonderful can be your future. You can still flourish in all of your future tomorrows. For me, having peace of mind has been a great reward for my efforts. Why my childhood had to be the way that it was is a question I may never be able to answer. I have yet to make full sense of those cruel days. Nevertheless, I learned along the way that I was created with enough positive power in my humanity to confront the nightmares of the past and end the relentless mental anguish that was cutting off my access to happiness and left my spirit exhausted. I had to learn in the most difficult of ways that no one who keeps standing on a foundation built by emotional pain will ever be raised to positive newness. There is no kind of good lasting inspiration in the indulgence of self pity. The other chance I needed was in my still beating heart. Giving up hope all together and allowing sadness to perish me would have been far worst than the abuse that was applied to my formative years. We are wrong about so many of the things we do to each other and to this planet of ours. It would be so wonderful if all human beings all over the world would, in spite of the color of our skin, could see the great miracle in a single breath. It is unfortunate that we take each other for granted. Some of us flat out refuse to respect our own humanity. If we all applied love instead of hatred and brutality, can you take a moment to imagine how much more beautiful this world would be? The solution for a more peaceful existence will always lie with us. There is an enormous abundance in love and kindness. It is a pleasantness that can travel through millions of miles. Thinking about this fact always leaves me wishing there were more kindness in the world among the race. Making the decision to live a happier life could benefit so many people. When sadness is allowed to envelope even one person permanently, it is such a great loss to the world. You have so many reasons to love yourself, whether you realize it or not. You may see yourself as imperfect, but the creator of the universe sees you as one made perfectly. You are a great gift from a merciful and gracious God. God is a patient God, but we should all live with the constant reminder that our days are borrowed. Make haste to live in the miracles of your life. Run to the powerful goodness that awaits you. Embrace your life eagerly instead of treating yourself with contempt because you were once touched by evil hands. Use your built-in God given power and refuse to let evil acts influence you. Don't let them decide for you. When these troubled memories come calling, refuse to answer. Instead, recall the most ecstatic moments you can remember, even the ones from your fantasies. Smile. Laugh at or with them. This is just one of the things that can help you cope in times when you feel as if you might revert to the disturbing memories of yesterday. There are many ways to a more peaceful life, but none as powerful as faith. If you have faith in the power that gave you life, you are far from being alone. Better tomorrows await. Faith is far more reliable than we are. Whatever the Jehovah does, He is never in error. Nothing on earth can set things straighter than a faithful prayer. I speak from experience. As much as the creator understands us better than we understand ourselves, we do not need Him to tell us that sadness is not a pathway we should take. Our wrong ideas about the ways in which we should treat ourselves and each other have always been a stumbling block. The things we decide without the benefit of practical wisdom often leads to costly failings. If you could see and understand all of the reasons for your creation, you would be so impressed. Why not be impressed anyway, with all of the good things you already know about yourself. Why not see and appreciate how much you matter in this world. You are the only you that you have. Whether you like yourself or not, you will have to do. You can find the true happiness that will benefit your life if you are willing to faith your way to a new way of life. Sadness should not flow through you for the rest of your life. The only other thing besides the blood flowing through your veins that should flow through you forever is the power of the Almighty. Sadness and depression is the most careless company any innocent victim of abuse could choose to keep. There is only one perfect reliable Source of peace. Use it as you do living waters. Your value as a human being here on this earth extends far beyond your internal conflicts. All of your thoughts and intentions are known to the most high. That is why it is wise to keep in mind our intentions can be used to our benefit or be used against us. If your intention, your prayer is to live a better life, the Master of the universe is already calling it done. And it will be long before your prayers are completed. The results from the prayers we pray asking for miracles sometimes work in the same way that the herbal medicine created by love does. We don't always see the results right away, in spite of the fact that it starts doing what it was meant to do right away. It is slow, but gives good results that are more permanent. The result of a sincere prayer is always beneficial in the ways God decides is best for us. Your life was not created by a loser. You were created by the original Genius. Skillfully made, you are an impressive reality of love, a magnificent creation that came straight from the heart of God. You are a work of heart, a classic work of art. To reject yourself is to reject the creator of life. Obviously, it is in your best interest not to limit your joy. If you are not doing what is best for your own life, you cannot offer your best to anyone else. You cannot give what you don't have to give. Replacing your true self with grief is never a solution for anyone. No one can live well in grief. With your agreement, you can break away from the "I must live sad" mentality. It is possible to make better provisions for your soul. You can start today to grow out of your despair and live a happy, healthy, fruitful life. There should always be a boundary between prolonged sadness and the human heart, a boundary that should never be crossed. In spite of the ugliness that we see in our world, the earth we live on today was given to us as a paradise to dwell in peace. We should all examine our lives as never before. You are a wonderful earthly purpose meant to be filled with happiness. A horrible experience you had yesterday should not be allowed to rob you of today. It should not hold back the good things from your life. Abusers of the innocent are not only criminals; they are insults that should not continue challenging you. There is a very satisfying way to live. You do not have to continue living under the influence of satan's worshippers. Do not accept those bad remembrances as your ruler. You did not invite sinful humans to harm you. Let them be the ones to bang their heads against the rocks. It's time for you to open up your life to an overflow of blessings. Why continue to remain back there in those bitter childhood days. There are a billion better ways to feel alive. There's no need to sacrifice your entire life to pain. The roads of your life should not be paved with pain. It is not too late to love and respect yourself enough to provide a shelter of peace for your weary soul. Believe me when I tell you that first steps are a lot easier than condemning yourself to "too late." It is impossible to live your best life when your very thoughts are being controlled by violent memories. You will never find your wholeness until you become your favorite thing to love and embrace. The intervention of love of self and the respect that comes with that can take you to the necessary wiser living that is so much a part of the good energy needed for wholeness. You can become a perfect example of how God intended for us to live and how to treat each other. Yes, it is true that reaching beyond the worst of emotional pain is never an easy reach. Yet it is possible to find your way out of this prison and take part in the best that life has to offer. You can get to that place in your life where you can recognize the big chance in the greatness of your humanity and bloom brilliance forever. There is no end to the great things you can accomplish, no end to the blessings you will receive. The breath of life is the finest example of privilege that there is. Despite my sufferings, I am truly grateful to have been spared the worst that sadness has to offer. Many tortured souls were faithful to sadness until death. The corrupt gathering of evil remembrances was allowed to take away their mortality way too soon. Peace for the human soul while still living in the flesh is not a new idea. It is your birth right. You can have that peaceful existence. You should have peace starting right now, today. Having a peaceful soul is the greatest reward for the flesh that there is. The true value of peace is so powerful it could save the entire world from destruction. That's how much it is worth. Let it begin in your soul today. Give it as a valuable gift to yourself. You will find yourself expressing the great joy you feel inside. Refuse to suffer at the hands of enemies anymore. You are not anyone's dog. Refuse to give up your life opportunity. This is your one chance to do what is best for your life. Refuse to be nailed to the cross that you were given to bear. You have been tortured enough. Let hell fend for itself. Don't be a part of it anymore. Get out while you can. Stop giving power to the toxic emotions that are hell bent on destroying the best of your humanity. No toxic emotion can destroy you unless you make room for it in your life and give it your permission to do so. Right now, this day you can rise up into the positive power in you and begin a journey of miracles you had no idea was waiting for your enjoyment. A renewed spirit can be very rewarding. It is possible to restore your life to what the same power that created the heavens and the earth intended for it to be. Mental anguish is not inescapable. There is a way forward. Rise each morning with the knowledge you are a celebration of life itself. Lose no more of yourself. Refuse to be reduced to emotional weakness. Keep your mind above garbage. Never allow it free reign again. You have the divine resources that you need already weaved into the fiber of your being. Power it up and dedicate yourself to joy. Refuse to let anyone minimize your positive power. If you are a decent human being living a God-fearing life, there is no one in this world that is more significant than you. I don't care how many pricy earthly possessions they have. In spite of the abuse suffered, you are still as good and as valuable a human being as anyone else. The earthly possession outside of you is not how God determines your value as a human being. You are as precious to the Almighty as anyone else is. It does not matter how different you feel your appearance is from other people. It does not diminish your value as a human being. The intentions of your heart are how the greatest Power that there is judges you. In spite of any disappointments that we may feel about our appearance, it does not take away from the perfect Power that created us. You are still jam-packed with the positive power that was used in your creation. Low self esteem has no business being in you. Pour it out instead of increasing your support for it. You have the power to pour it all out effectively. You are in charge. Why create mountains to climb? There is already more than enough of that in the world. Say goodbye to what ails your soul. You were created the complete opposite of toxic emotions. Stop including them. They defeat the purpose of your life. These services are not needed. Stop including these condemnations. You are not some leftovers to be cast aside. Your self image in your view is very different in God's view. Love yourself enough to stop the damaging effects of abuse. Be confident in the Savior's love. Use the wealth of inner strength you were given to eliminate the power of these remembrances. You have all the tools to do it. Your inner strength was created in you to be used to your benefit. Refuse to surrender any more of your life. Change your expectations to ones that are big, bold, and beautiful.

THE RICHNESS OF YOU

DON'T be ruled by fear. You can prevail in spite of life's real challenges. No matter how low you feel right now, you can still rise to a solid foundation if you are willing to start doing the things that are in your best interest. Let's face it, the world we live in does not offer us any kind of iron clad security. All the more reason we should care about our mental health. Our intentions where our mental health is concerned should always be peaceful ones. This is the most reasonable we can request of ourselves. We should never allow outside influences to reverse the blessings for our life. Living a comfortable, peaceful life should not be as difficult as we have made it for ourselves. There are difficulties inflicted by cruel circumstances that we have the power to go beyond and make better sense of our lives. There are areas of our lives that we place an element of caution unnecessarily so that, in turn, we can keep us from living our best life. Not everyone is conscious of the self-inflicted wounds that often take place because of the toxic belief one is less valuable. Because of the abuse suffered, there is an abandonment of self that can happen without realization, not until it's too late or until too much damage has been done to reverse the effects of self abuse. Preservation of self is very important, especially after surviving the awful reality of abuse. Take better care of yourself. Your heart deserves that much from you. It is because of the short time that we are allowed to live why we can not afford to keep getting it wrong. Not everyone sees it that way. Nevertheless, it is still a serious fact. Every time someone dies that we did not expect to die so suddenly, it is a warning to the rest of us not to take the gift of life for granted. Surely everyone old enough to understand what the end of life means should be able to use this fact as a reason to live peacefully. We don't have enough time for severe self punishment. Common sense alone is enough to work with to start the process of emotional healing. Being a problem to yourself is quite frankly an insane way to live. Some people feel that the only way to despair is to do it long term. Believe me, this kind of mentality will not get you up; it will only work to set your life aside and put everything else that you cherish in serious jeopardy. There is strong evidence depression is humans' worst exploration. It is not a place I want to see again. Millions of people get lost there forever. I feel so blessed to have escaped with my dignity. For the rest of my life, I will protect my soul from harm whenever possible. I refuse to continue living in the frightful days of the past. In spite of everything, use peace to nourish your soul. Your life does not have to be all doom and gloom. The almighty did not assign you to grief. You were not born to live in permanent ruin. A peaceful, joyful life is the only life that should capture and hold your attention forever. If you had made yourself, you would not be such a magnificent creation. Don't make yourself miserable. You can make yourself better than that. After all, God has already given you His best, the gift of life. Trust that you have in your life the greatest, most powerfully perfect undying love that there is. Sometimes circumstances make that difficult to believe, especially on those cruel occasions when we feel as if we have been captured in a net of unending disasters that leave our mind, heart and soul feeling scorched. I assure you, none of it is Jehovah's intent. We are still His privileged children with the same unlimited access to miracles no matter how many times life takes us by surprise. Press on in spite of life's unpleasant surprises. The power of the Almighty can raise you above any wreckage. Your life need not be a permanent complicated mess. Oppression need not be a part of your journey. The very fact that living in a state of sadness is not a role specifically designed by our Creator should tell us that it is not a wise or healthy way to live. At the core of our being, we know this to be a fact. Yet some of us are still willing to ignore this fact. Don't you think we should all live with more concern for our emotional well being as we do our physical well being? Interestingly enough, as bad as living in a state of constant sadness is for the human entire being, there are people who flat out refuse to give it up. They have become accustomed to it and feel it is their right to do so in spite of the fact that it is not a well being emotion. To give up their deep sadness would be to remove what might be the only reason they have to feel sorry for themselves. A lot of people are afraid of any kind of change. I made a decision some years back for myself that has served me well over the years and continues to do so. And that is, I would rather die laughing than die crying. As a little girl, before the indecent assaults on my life, I enjoyed laughing even though I was being raised in an environment I knew in my little heart was not right for my soul or for my body. Somewhere along the journey of my growing up years, the laughter died. Life for me lost its true flavor, and even though I could still feel my heart beating, I was not alive in the other ways that counted. I was not living my best life. I was merely existing. My mind was not mine alone. The part that was stolen I had yet to retrieve. The poisonous legacy was still very much a part of my humanity. Scared and naïve, I had no idea how or where to begin to take back my life. As loudly as I was screaming on the inside, no one could hear me, and even if they could there was no one in my environment with the know-how to help me. Your life should be beautifully big. It should be everything you dreamed it could be. You have a responsibility to yourself to be happy. Please don't accept a life of sadness as the only way to live because of past unfairness. Those cruel facts should not be given the power to control your life. Your God given power should not be shared this way. It is all yours to use to your benefit. There are extraordinary benefits in having peace of mind. The process from sadness to joy is not as difficult a transition as you might think. There is no good reason to fear a peaceful life. I was taught through brute force how to disappoint myself, but in spite of this cruelty, I have learned to look at the broader significance of my life. Gone are the days when I would put on a brave face in spite of the inner turmoil to try and fool myself and others that all was well with my soul. That brave face I wore when I though it necessary to do so was not enough. There is no healing in pretending. I had to change how I saw myself, how I viewed the world, and my place in it. I could not afford to continue allowing the memories of abusers with their history of violent aggression to continue ripping my mind apart. I had to refuse to help them spread destruction, and I am determined to keep it that way for as long as I walk the earth. I will not be forced to pay for anyone else's evil with my own life. What's mine is mine. I will not live in a bind. Those guilty of the most horrible misconduct are the ones whose mind should be experiencing torture, not yours. Your incredible abilities are needed. Although you might have suffered greatly, your heart still beats with the everlasting love it was created from. You have the power to keep the cruelest of surprises from taking away your most precious gift, you. You can get it right. Pain does not have to keep slicing up your life. You are a profound gift of love. More kindness to yourself will help to heal psychological damage. What's too heavy you don't have to carry. Desire more success for yourself. Embrace peace, and trust that Jehovah can deliver the right justice. Living with the constant pounding of mental anguish is a horrible way to live. I know this all too well. It was mental anguish that almost robbed me of my remaining breaths. I was drawn into the deepest, darkest zone of sadness. Each time I used the power of my mind to journey back to the awful childhood truths, I hated the results of these trips that left my entire life parched. I was so thirsty for what no one else could give me, freedom from the worst of remembrances, the kind of peaceful human freedom that was already mine for the accepting. All I had to do was love myself to freedom. It's a pathway I did not understand how to take. Instead, I felt like a prison inmate stuck with a massive ball and chain. When it came to escaping the worst of memories, I had no know-how. I lived my life fearing each tomorrow's forecast. I had no idea what day or hour of the day I would allow those horrible memories to terrorize me again. I felt demolished each time I used those horrible memories to assault not only my senses, but by entire being. The recollections had me spiraling out of control. My self worth was not being realized, and since I thought I had no cushion against the fast fist from the past and no place that I could run to, I just accepted the surge of grief as though it were a natural human passage. I thought it was the price I had to pay for being human. It was as if I could be human no other way. Without my full realization, those childhood nightmare experiences left me believing that for me life was devoid of choices, that I had to be sad if I wanted to remain human. That kind of toxic mentality is a full heavy load of garbage. Some who were abused or are being abused are dragging it around with them. Someone with low moral fiber, crap clouded judgments, unnatural urges, and no respect for the precious gift of human life altered the course of your life by violating your trust, a nasty betrayal that as a result dumped so much garbage on your life that the weight of it all pushed you out of your rightful place in this world. Some of us are not even aware of the negative adjustments that the old sins kept alive forced us to make. For some the belief that I am not as valuable as those other fellow human beings not touched by abuse, is so strong and so deeply rooted, it is difficult to notice the toxic fed branches quietly spreading out into their environment and fulfilling the desires of the monster or monsters who planted the seeds for garbage in your mind in the first place. No good decent soul should be shaded by garbage. This ugly dangerous altered state of mind will only continue to provide nourishment for the seeds of evil. In this altered state of mind you will continue to doubt the important aspects of your life. Don't accept anyone's bad behavior, past or present, as something you have to put up with. We are called adults when we are old enough to be wise. The kinds of bad behaviors that I am referring to do not apply to children. Children need our guidance. I am talking about not accepting any kinds of bad behavior from adults who are old enough to know better but who use abuse as a way of controlling another person they feel is too weak to defend themselves. I am not sure if there is anyone anywhere on this planet who truly understands the mindset of an abusive deviant. So don't waste any more of your time wondering why you. Your body and your mind is your own personal private refuge. No one had a right to invade. But keeping those old toxic memories on stand-by is a handy way of robbing yourself of the joy, of the peace you need as you journey through this life. You no longer have to cooperate. Refuse to go along with anything that is pulling your life apart. Don't put up with it. Refuse to be lessened. If you don't things are not going to get any better. I don't believe that life should include the suffering that comes as the result of abuse. Without meaning to, many victims of abuse end up losing that crucial ability to think independently. I call that the "Frog in the Pot" syndrome. They had no idea when things took a turn for the worse. There are no perfect human families; we know that. No matter how much some of us pretend that there are, we know in our hearts that there is no such thing as a perfect family. There are families that are much better behaved than others. There are families who pretend to be better than others. And there are families that are not afraid or ashamed to let the rest of the world see how terrible they are. Perhaps you are from one of those dysfunctional families that look perfectly peaceful to the entire world, yet there is full blown hell in the middle. If this is the kind of environment in which you were raised, you must ask yourself if seeing ugly human behavior in your formative years makes it easier for you to accept your life as an adult. After years of advancing into wisdom and excelling in my mental health, I heard myself say, if hell is even one degree worst than what I was forced to endure in my childhood, it is certainly a place that I will do whatever it takes not to have to experience. Those of us who came face-to-face with evil at an early age, and has suffered as a result of the bad actions of others has an even bigger obligation to do what is in our best interest, not for a week, a month, a year, but for the rest of our lives. Every morning that I am still blessed to wake up, I consider myself the new release. I feel so blessed that I am no longer imprisoned by remembrances that had no real power over me. The only power they had over me were the power I gave to them. I was responsible for releasing them back into my life. I allowed these painful reflections frequent visits, as if I had no mental control as I sold my soul to them. I am not ashamed to tell you that my escape was a narrow one. The seriousness of how I was allowing past wrongs to influence my most important life's decisions came in the knick of time to spare my remaining days from a miniature life. The benefits of having peace of mind keep increasing. Giving yourself the gift of inner peace will be fantastic. You will never regret it, but most importantly, Jehovah guarantees it. There are more than enough miracles for you too. Despite how cruel circumstance might have affected your mind and your life, it is not the end. Turn your attention to new beginnings. Forget about any growing negative demands. That is not the way to fulfill your destiny because such demands are not your destiny. You are bigger than that. You are better than that. There are extraordinary safe healthy places in your mind that you can visit instead. You don't need any kind of negative connections. Move your life to a safer place so that you can enjoy your remaining days. Your life means something bigger than even you realize. Get started on your healthier larger life. Your efforts will not be in vain. Your destiny is for greatness. Put an end to the domination. You are a hope that you can bring to any of life's challenges. And far more than just a glimmer, you are a major source. There is an abundance of love to tap into. It does not matter how small your adult body is. You can still make a big difference in your own life as well as in the lives of people who could use a little encouragement from someone like yourself who might have suffered as you did. You have that in your power. You also have within your power the ability to start the process of regeneration. Every faithful change will allow you to do good for yourself. I am sure every human being who has ever suffered as a result of being wronged knows that sadness is not a peaceful sanctuary. When it comes to your right to have peace, don't accept anything less, the Creator wants only the very best for us. If it were not so when He restores it would not always be so accurate. The imperfections that were forced into your human experience do not mean that is all life has to offer you. I have learned over the years what a big difference one human being can make in this world. If one, just one single abusive deviant can cause so much pain, can you imagine how much joy a good person like yourself can spread throughout this world? Try it, you will see what I mean. The results will amaze you. And you will get even better at it each time you spread a little love, a little joy, a little sunshine in someone else's life. I have found that it is a beautiful way to focus those good energies. It will provide new courage you can also use in other areas of your life. Each new courageous act that benefits others will be ones you can reap the most rewards from. You will wish you had discovered that side of you before. You will hear yourself say time and time again, I didn't know I had it in me. You do because you were made that way. You will find that this is the natural you. You were not born withdrawn, nor were you born to spend the rest of your life struggling to get out from under. God is more experienced than that. The Creator of your life has the most powerful, the most unique insight that there is. He did not create anything to be buried alive under the weight of evil. The master of the universe only created survival souls. See yourself as the survival type and use faith in the power greater than yourself to shatter your deepest sadness. If you are one who were physically and emotionally harmed, it is important to always remember that the fact that you were abused by a bully with false courage does not mean your Creator's intention for your life was to make you a target for evil. Abusers are selfish human beings. It is that selfishness that leads them to be abusive to the precious sacred gift of life. It is a disgusting desire to dominate. The last thing that an insecure, selfish, evil, abusive person thinks about is the fact that they too are only dust. They find the gift of freewill easy to abuse. The type of selfishness born from their evil thought and desires and the abuse of their God given freewill are just a few of the reasons your soul was crucified. And perhaps you are the one who experienced the worst abuse while your brain was still wiring and have been left since your formative years to suffer alone. Because of my own hellish childhood experiences, I cannot help asking the question. If some of those people in authority over the lives of innocent little children have no respect for their own lives and is setting that example, how then can we expect those children to understand how to value and respect their own lives? The following request is well worth being made again. If you are an innocent victim of abuse, with every breath that you take, please bear in mind you did not invite it. Abuse is what it is. You were dragged into the line of fire. As sickening as it is, there are human beings among us who enjoy preying on their fellow human beings. Unfortunately for the rest of us, there are human beings on our planet that cannot go a single day without causing trouble for someone else, as you know. These disturbing fellow human beings live to destroy. Of course they do have it within their power not to be destructive, but instead, they prefer to live in full support of evil's forces. Spending every waking moment plotting to take unfair advantage of anyone they are able to take advantage of. Some of their victims are forced to play nice while suffering inner deaths. I know this to be a fact because this was what I had to do as a child to avoid the angriest blows from my abusers, blows to my small still growing body that could have ended my life. For me, at such a young age it was in my best interest to do whatever was necessary to survive. Believe me, it took a lot to survive. In spite of the deep hatred I felt for the ignorant, selfish, barbaric abusive monsters in my environment, I knew I could not express my deep contempt.

To do so would have no doubt cost me my life. The only tool I had in my possession against the human weapons that formed against my innocent young life was prayer. It was the one good thing that I could do for myself right in the presence of my enemies without them knowing I was talking to God about them. Every prayer that I prayed I was sure in my heart that God Himself would figure out a way to rescue me from the abusers of my flesh and soul. When the results I prayed for did not happen right away for me, I became very angry with God and hated my abusers even more. I knew in my heart I did not belong in that environment, but I was still only a child left with no other choice but to continue playing nice with a heart filled with hate for what was so cruel and unfair. I realized years later, long after I was finally rescued by my Creator's mercy from this hell that my desperate and sincere prayers had been answered long before my heart completed them. I also came to realize how truly wise this ultimate power is. I am not the only one who was angry at the selfish, cold-blooded, heartless abusers. God was angry too. And He was not only on my side; He was beside me all along. He saw my blood as it flowed from my mouth. He saw my tears, and He heard my prayers. God has a habit of setting things right, but He does it in His own time, not in ours. I am another living proof that prayer changes things. Even a little can add up to a lot. No matter how brief, each sincere prayer is that you pray the accumulative effect will result in many surprising miracles. In your adult life, if you are an able-bodied person who is able to remove yourself from abuse, you should not be accepting it as the only way to live. You never have to accept an abusive situation as your only option. Have faith that you can take back your life from the dreadfulness, and move on to the life your Creator approved for you. No matter how horrible your childhood was, you should not be living with the belief that abuse is all that life has to offer you. Choosing to accept abuse is the wrong choice. It is a horrible choice. If today is just not the right day for you to start respecting and loving yourself enough to say, there is not way in hell I am going to continue allowing myself to be dehumanized, then when? Remaining in any kind of abuse situation lessens your chances of receiving the gift of tomorrow. Please take that fact into consideration before you decide to keep putting your life on hold, especially if the hand of abuse is really what's holding it. Your urgent effort is needed. Those of us who were abused as children should never waste precious time as adults comparing monsters. The monster who is abusing you now might not be quite as bad as the ones in your childhood, but a monster is a monster. Remove your life from this cycle. It is only fair you allow yourself the opportunity to experience a peaceful way of life. You have but one chance to live in this life. While you have breath, while you are still walking under God's heaven, while you can see today, start protecting your own one and only life chance. Don't lower yourself to what an abusive deviant said you were. Your soul was not created to be assaulted by other human beings with no respect for life. Don't allow those echoes from the past to lower your life by fooling you into believing you must continue to accept abuse into your life. Even as an adult, you do not have to accept this as your fate, not under any circumstances in any way, shape or form. Your abusers will never value you. Your duty to yourself is to put the matter straight. Start with the fact that you are not less valuable as a human being because you were or are being abused. You are not responsible for the sins of monsters past or present. That cross is not for you to carry. Remaining in any kind of abusive situation sends the wrong message, and if you are one of us who were also abused in your formative years, recalling those memories can sometimes be more than enough to make an unpleasant difference in your day. I honestly believe there would be far less people involved in substance abuse if they were blessed with an emotionally healthy childhood environment. Unfortunately, there are millions of substance abusers in the world, some of whom became what they are because they are desperately trying to erase the past from their memories, memories that are still being given the power to haunt them. Some substance abusers eventually succeed in erasing those painful haunting memories, but only after they have erased themselves as well. As someone who has been slammed by abuse, I know how lethal these memories can be, if they are allowed the advantage. Being too mentally and physically tired from recalling the ugliness of the past is not always enough to help some victims of abuse to find the peace that their souls need. For many years, I took the worst of memories to bed with me every night and allowed them to torment and brutalize my mind.

And for a time, it was a fate I was willing to accept until I realized what a terrible burden and a curse on my precious life those memories were. Please don't wait for a health crisis to realize how precious your own gift of life is. You are not a zone for war. Get living the right way. You will find it divinely refreshing. No good person should have to journey through life with a knot of fear in their gut. It is only fair that in spite of monsters you live with a joy filled heart. There is no question about it. Emotional expression is a permanent part of who we are, but I don't believe constant emotional pain should be included. Your life should be a lot better than that. Toxic emotions will always keep you from applying the right kinds of generosity to your life. Living with toxic emotions is really no way to live. Yes, I know how difficult it can be for some people to live without the memories of sick monsters being a part of your daily life, but it is possible to keep those memories from controlling your life without going to harmful extremes. The horrible victimization does not have to continue at your own hands. You should not be spending precious days waiting to be assaulted by those memories. It's a waste of time that you can stop wasting. Ask yourself this. Who is going to reimburse you for a wasted life? Where can you go to sign up to have those wasted days refunded? You know as I do there is no way to get those days back after they have been wasted to grief. It's impossibility. No one has ever been able to retrieve a single moment. Cruel distant past should remain in the past. Keeping them close to your life will certainly keep you from thriving. There are people right at this moment whose feelings of anger and helplessness are what are causing them to abuse themselves in whatever form of abuse they choose. Big mistake. Believe me, I do know how close those distant memories can come when they have the permission they need for destruction. No question about it, you have the power to raise your life above them. You have the inner strength to push out the wrong ideas about yourself that you were forced through abuse to adopt. You can stop thinking of yourself as having less value. Keep this in your mind with every breath that you take. The very fact that you were given the precious gift of life means that you arrived authorized to value yourself.

REINFORCING YOURSELF

You were not created to live beyond the reach of happiness. Some victims of abuse withdraw from life all together, living terrified of trusting. Fear has been given permission to take away their courage to trust anyone, themselves included. They have lost the courage needed to trust anyone enough to share their lives. They don't believe they could choose someone who would not betray their trust. Many victims of abuse feel safer behind the brick walls that they have built for themselves. And of course these emotional brick walls are not easily torn down. I know this to be a fact. The ones I built for myself were far more solid than I realized. Even so, I was still able to escape with dignity. I have no regrets. Those were not the walls that I needed to protect my soul. My deep sadness was not sent from heaven; it was instead a hellish way to live. Many people's installation into sadness is very solid with no intention of discovering or recovering their true identity. They are living with a mind set that they consider the perfect solution. You don't have to get to that point in your life when you don't listen to your heart and soul anymore. Your concentration should never be removed from what's in your best interest. The things in life that are bad for the human soul should never be allowed to represent you. You do have the inner strength to face challenges without giving up on your own life. You can confront unpleasantness and still keep your sanity in tact. You are able to wake up tomorrow morning and say, "What a great evidence of miracles I am," and really mean it. You are able to—as surely as you live and breathe. It will be fantastic. You will benefit greatly from this new attitude of faith. Liberty, liberty, liberty in your own positive ways should be a constant from now on. There is no time for snail's pace. Treat yourself to inner peace now, thou royal child of the earth. Allow faith and inner peace to show you the right path. Applying this daily freshness is sure to take your life further. You will be blessed. The unfortunate fact you were abused should not keep you from a healthy life for the rest of your life. Don't let a bad attitude force you to ignore the doors opened by God. You deserve more than a stagnant life. There is no limit to the blessing a new positive attitude will bring to your life. It takes inner peace to live your best life. The inability to trust because of past betrayals is not a best way to live. Notice I did not say it is wrong to be cautious and very selective when it comes to choosing those you include in your life. What I am saying is this. Isolation born from fear to trust does not provide a true allowance of joy. All you are doing is providing a jail cell for your mind. An allowance of joy is what should be a permanent part of your life. Your body is not the only thing you should be exercising. You should also be exercising the rightful positive freedoms of your humanity. I am not only grateful to have survived the worst blows to my body, I am also grateful for the realization that it is better to live wise and strong than weak and isolated. The important decisions in your life should not be made according to a low opinion of yourself. Life is a privilege that should never be taken for granted no matter how desperate you feel inside. Nothing should overshadow how truly precious you are. Honor and respect your life. It is, after all, by the grace of the Almighty that we are still alive. Any lousy relationship that you have should not be with yourself. It's unfair. You are the best earthly source for your most beautiful reality. Any lousy relationship that you have with yourself should be eliminated. You will be pleasantly surprised how enormous the pay off is for having the courage to do what is in your best interest. Indignities of any kind should be unacceptable to you. Any kind of delay in caring for your emotional health could lead to destruction. You are a lot stronger than you know. Give yourself the opportunity to find out how powerful you are. Your well being depends on your own conduct. Refuse to keep copying the belief of your attacker or attackers about the value of your life. You may not realize that you are, but that is what too many victims of abuse do, including myself at one time. As I mentioned earlier, I don't care who the person was who told you that you are not worth anything. If it were not God who told that you have no business still believing it. If you continue to believe the ugly words that were used to assault your soul and your mind, you cannot be as kind to yourself as you should be in the ways that matter most. You will, in fact, continue to have a lousy relationship with yourself, and that is not fair to you. Resolve to do something good for yourself for a change. Resolve to do whatever it takes to live a more peaceful life. Be as aggressive as you can be when pursuing inner peace. Resisting the urge to remain in the silence of sadness does not have to be futile. You will be so glad that you made the decision to live the rest of your life free from the controls of deep sadness. You will evolve and enjoy so much the feelings that result. Your highest running emotions should be joy-filled ones instead of horror filled ones. I am certain that having a life that is like a bad dream is not what you had in mind for yourself. Your life now as well as your future should match your positive potential. The injuries from emotional abuse can do to the human mind what you don't realize. Even so, what I pray that you will realize is the big difference that loving and respecting yourself can make in your mind, in your body and in your soul. Don't wait for time to tell you that you have not made the best of it. If you let your entire life be wasted looking back on yesteryears, and grieving over the unchangeable, you will long for the days when physical strength was on both of your sides. Abuse of any kind affects deeply. There is no question about that, but dividing your life up and giving the biggest piece to grief is not the Divine's plan for you. It's a destructive way to live. It's not how your life should be when your breath is finally taken away. Now is the time to carry and care for yourself as you would a newborn. We should never forget that life itself is the biggest chance that we have ever been given. Now that we are in possession of precious life, I believe we should live it with the same positive power it was given. You should see yourself everyday as the beautiful effort that was brought to life. Past or present, disappointments should never overpower and diminish the quality of your emotional health. Putting an end to inner struggles is not impossible.

There are as many excuses to live a life of deep sadness as there are people on the planet, but the fact remains, sadness or deep anger turned inward as depression has never really worked to anyone's benefit. It takes some of us longer than others to admit to ourselves that in spite of any horrific childhood experience, after we mature into adulthood, what we do with the precious gift of our life is up to us. We are one hundred percent accountable for the decisions that we make. You can transform the way that you live. You can have an amazing big beautiful life. Hell was brought to bear, but you should not have to bear it for the rest of your life. It's time for some outstanding growth. Growing power is yours. Unfairness should not be the thing growing in your life. Goodness and mercy should be placed back into your life with the powerful control of faith. Some people don't believe they can come out of a bad experience better and stronger than before. Giving yourself the opportunity to get caught up in faith will build you up. It is possible to stop mental pain from holding your life hostage. Past wrongs is the driving force in too many people's lives. Because of my own experiences with life's cruel disappointments, I can tell you that joining forces with faith is not as difficult as you might think. Fashioning a brand new, uniquely positive way of doing life is an experience that is sure to result in joyful rewards you will want to keep. Giving yourself an immediate increase in love should be done before you conclude you have been defeated. Look around you. There is inspiration in every living thing including you. Recognize this, and you will find that no matter how low you feel, you are in your state of mind. There is still hope for the peace that will bring you better tomorrows. I have seen a lot of people who came out of some of the worst of experiences because they were determined to survive in spite of their many disappointments. I find their courage inspiring. They refused to give up without a fight or stand by and let life pass them by. No good human being can really afford to live sad, especially when we take into consideration that the fate of the entire world lies with us. The fate of every other living thing is in our hands. They need all of us. That is all the more reason for us to love and respect ourselves in spite of the selfish evil fellow human beings among us. Think about this for a moment. If we as human beings cannot respect our own lives and the lives of others, what will the fate of this planet and the other life forms that inhabit it be? I am mindful that not everyone had the good fortune to receive the gift of this brand new day. I don't know if you are as glad as I am for the remarkable gift of today. It is a miracle I could only imagine yesterday.

I am always grateful to be included in the gift of each new day. In the past when I would tell people that I see each new day as miracle central, they would suddenly begin looking at me in a strange way. I always knew what the question was that would follow the strange looks. Miracle what? They would ask me as if they just could not believe their ears. Back then as it remains true today, I was always more than happy to repeat those words as well as explained what I meant by "miracle central." The fact that you are blessed to be alive. This day puts you in the center of other miracles that are as limitless as your potentials. As long as you have breath, regardless of what it is that you don't like about your body, wonderful things are still possible for you. Life has endless joyful rewards, but you must be open to them so you won't miss out. I speak from my own personal experiences when I tell you that any kinds of deep anger or sadness left in control of your life will continue to invite other unpleasantness. It is not only the mind that depression hurts. If left to have its way with you, it will destroy the best of who you are. Most people who are living in a state of deep sadness would not want to be murdered. Yet that is exactly what they are doing to themselves in a slow painful way. If you went for a drive in the country and you came upon a sign that said "approaching danger," you would stop or at least slow down, would you not? You would not want to ignore the warning and risk making a fatal mistake. Ignoring your emotional health could prove costly. Why make difficulties for yourself? Life is tough enough at times. When God created you, He did not see you as a careless investment. Every ounce of the true value of your life belongs to you. In this powerful circle of life that you are a part of, every positive contribution that you are able to make will never be wasted efforts. Whether it is to your own life or to the lives of fellow human beings, you will be greatly rewarded. Be prepared. There are blessings in every positive contribution, blessings that will astound you. Sometimes the worst kinds of oppression that we experience are self-inflicted. A wonderful variety of life experiences is missed when we are lost. A life of torment and pressure should not be desirable to anyone. The human spirit cannot soar under such bad conditions. Loyalty to unpleasantness is a misguided way to live. Get seriously brilliant and start living excellence. Fun in your life should not be a mere chance encounter. When you smile, it should not come as a surprise to you. For too many people a toxic past still carries with it the power to erode, all the more reason why it cannot hurt to seek the help of a mental health professional. For many people, this is a necessary helping hand to make sure the wrong tools are not used to remove the mental anguish. At the same time if you are ready and willing to reach for the positive power in you, you can deal with adversity as you would the cold-blooded monster who first introduced you to it. You were not created as a vessel to carry pain all the days of your life. Don't let anyone force you to be a pain collector. Before anyone can consider you over and done with, please give the following some thought. You were not created as a resting place for evil. That is a fact. It is also a fact that you are greatness born, a spirit that was reconstructed to flesh for a temporary earthly experience, and another reason why a single moment of evils consequences paid by an innocent human being is far too cruel. Each breath that you take should be allowed its sweet independence. They should be as free as the first ones you took. The breaths taken without your full appreciation is not as sweet. It's like having cleaner air which is perfectly wonderful, but appreciating it makes the benefits even better. No one needs the crushing contaminants of abuse—no one! It is very important to pay close attention to what you are doing to your own life. Rewinding the past for anything less than joyful remembrances is costing you valuable time you cannot afford. Living an emotionally, unstable life as the result of being abused is not an affordable choice. For a great number of people, this often leads to loneliness. That loneliness then leads to despair. Shutting down your life because of a cruel experience will only work to maximize the pain. You don't need that. The only thing you should be maximizing is life's beautiful benefits. Many of which are available to you right this minute. You don't necessarily have to start with big things. A few joyful steps will help get you started with the right restructuring of your life. Things must change if you are to live a peaceful life. The acceptance of mental laboring must end. The rubbish must be removed no matter how unbearably heavy and "stuck with it" it may seem. You do have the ability to survive and get out from under this weight.

You need not carry it forever. The rubbish must go! The greatest investment that you can make is in your own peace of mind. Thinking about the good things you would like to do for yourself is not going to do you much good unless you act on it before it's too late. No matter how racked you are with emotional pain or with regrets for the wrong choices you have made as a result of an abusive past, there is always a better alternative. No human being that is drowning in sadness can make the most of each sunrise. One of the most powerful things that you can do for your life is to renew your spirit. If you were to promise to really do better for yourself and actually keep that promise, you would be thrilled when you see how well things turn out for you. When it comes to loving and caring for your body and soul, anything that is not a positive contribution is totally unnecessary. Your best reinforcement here on earth is your mind. So if it's preoccupied with grief, you are not as awesome, not as superb as you should be. Grief removes all of your top qualities. Sadness is one of the worst ways that you can share yourself. Keep in mind, there is only one spotless Lamb of God. Human beings make mistakes. Most human beings on this planet make bad choices we wish we could go back and change. That's no secret, but what might still be a secret to you is how powerful you are. You might feel empty, but you are not. When it comes to your mental health, you don't have to keep coming up empty. Divorce yourself from the negative twines. Rubbish will never count for eternal significance. Don't ignore the reality of how special you are. If you don't waste your life, you won't be left needing it back. A life of sadness is not a fate you have to accept. Color yourself free from torments. True peace must come from within. Peace is as valuable as your own life. Neither can be bought.

Become more attached to your own inner strength. Discover the gift of power in your possession given by the greatest Thinker. Discovering these truths will broaden any narrow vision that you might have of yourself. Think how wonderful it would be if you allowed yourself to experience the better you. Yes, there is an even better you yet to be discovered by you. You are a giant against killer thoughts and emotions. Stamp them down. Bring about the peace your soul so thirsts for. It is because there is only one you. That's why putting an end to the human sacrifice mentality before the rising of the next dawn is so important. Time is simply running out on us. Who could fault you for being in a hurry to live your best life now?

I was forced to spend years of my teens feeling as if I were a litter box for demons fresh from Satan's laboratory. My abusers were totally and completely out of order, and that is exactly where they dragged my young mind. Mine was a mind dragged out of the peacefulness it was created to exist in. It is because of my own experiences with vicious wretches why I can tell you that any kind of bad conditions in your life today should not be allowed to plague your mind. Some adults who were forced to experience a lot of garbage in their formative years tend to lose compassion for themselves in the areas of their lives where it matters the most. Some people might say that those people are just living boring lives, but I see it differently. Some people who were abused in childhood end up living a life I see as unofficially a low paying life, which has nothing to do with wage earnings. What I mean by low paying life is, not getting the joy out of your life that you should, remaining stuck in the darkness instead of allowing yourself to journey into the spiritual light of strength and courage. You don't have to continue being a victim of your own self doubt. Your life and the greatest power in the universe are interconnected. Cold hearts were not given to human kind. It is our very own ungodly thoughts that make it so. Nevertheless, in spite of the cold thoughts that were brought to bear broken spirits can be made whole again. You can emerge fearless and full of motivation. Nothing can justify allowing mental anguish to inhabit your mind long term. Why live incapacitated in any way, shape or form if you don't have to? If you must label yourself make it a powerfully good one that will be an inspiration to others. Don't remain undiscovered because you are living under the constant threat of toxic remembrances. You are the big positive difference that can be made in your life. Self doubt will keep lowering your life. You don't have to keep fighting a battle with the past. The fact that you have survived to see this day means that you have already won. Don't deny yourself freedom. You are not a failure. The loser who brought you horror is the failure. Become you again. Let your heart feel safe again. Improve your attention and live God's intentions for your life. Present yourself back to you in all the naturally beautiful ways of your Creator. Let the wonderful power of positivism come pouring back into you. Recognize the great fortune that you are and prefer it more. Combat insane memories, and be delicious. Refuse to let what weighs heavily keep you from being heavenly. Be the earthly light of your life. Take back your right to live a life free from the controls of evil. It's your life. Call it so. See it as such. If your Creator wanted you to spend your life being a dog, you would have been created a dog. Let your good dreams wake to their reality. Call your life in action to the higher place it belongs. Your quick actions will be enticing to your inner strength, accelerating your spiritual growth. There in your renewed spirit you will find an enormous amount of extra brain power that will help you meet life's difficulties faith on and win. You can remove the awful memories of rotten wretches from the center of your life and put them under your feet where they belong. It's time to put an end to the defeated mentality and start building on greater expectations of yourself. Don't be left starving for the better life you deserve. You have the right contacts in the faithful actions that will provide you more freedom. Faith in a power as great as the universe continues to be the fountain from which might miracles flow. Be wise, be the one to do miracles. Most often, they are not as difficult to get as you might think. Faith is a miracle magnet. Cruelty does not have to overpower you. When it comes to your well being, you cannot afford to support denial. It's way too costly. Nor can you afford to waste a moment of your short span. Exercise your right to have the best relationship with your soul that is possible. It's your journey, make it fabulous. The fact that you might have stumbled or fallen is not an excuse to keep falling. You are far more powerful than the dirt you might have fallen into. You don't have to stay down. Get back up and show hell who's boss. You are a heavenly link, you are not weak. Some people are actually afraid to succeed in the areas of their lives that matters the most because of the resentments and enemies that having a successful life can sometimes bread. If you are one of those people holding your life back for fear of losing friends or family to resentment and/or shameless expressions of jealousy, don't despair. The people who truly love you whole-heartedly will encourage your success instead of speaking ill of you. So fear not. Moving on to a more successful life is one of the best ways to weed out resentful jealous people. The shock of your success will force them to show you exactly who they really are. Removing your life from the choking weeds will work to your blessings. Living your life to please everyone else except you is unfair to you. What others desire of you should not be robbing you of a peaceful comfortable life. Accepting a stagnant life as your fate in order to accommodate your abuser could result in an extremely painful finish. There is no reason to keep fracturing your life by including yourself in the evil untidiness of others. If you do not value you enough to want to renew your own life, the future will pay a heavy toll for the past. No matter how deep in the emotional pain is, it is still possible to find peace of mind. Removing the pain from your life won't leave you powerless or empty just with enough room to grow. No one should keep alive those pieces of the past you have no positive use for. Negative flashbacks will hold your life back. Those negative flashbacks won't offer you any hope for tomorrow, and they certainly won't help you to realize the value of your own life. Tumbling helplessly into a well of sadness will not offer you the great quality of life that you deserve. You are alive now. That is cause for celebration. What you should always live mindful of is the fact that you were included into life with a specific purpose. Finding out what that purpose is, is far more difficult to do if you are too sad to make the right spiritual contributions to your soul. Life is not meant to be a ceremony of sadness. The end to your sadness can be found in your willingness to reach for the positive power in you and embrace peace. We know all too well that there are millions of our fellow human beings who, regardless of their past cruelty to others, continue to live in a sinful fashion. I've reminded you of that in the hopes of bringing about for you the realization of how bad it would be for you to waste your entire lifetime waiting for those who abused you to tell you how sorry they are for the crimes committed against you before you can move on with the rest of your life. It is a fact that most criminals after committing their crimes never give it a second thought. They go right on living their lives without a care in the world, as if they did nothing wrong. They go right on laughing, not losing a minute of sleep, just living their lives to the fullest while you remain impaled on emotional pain. The horrible mental anguish they left you, robbing you of a good nights rest, stuck right there where they wanted you to be.

While you are left suffering, they are living it up in a big way. You are not a concern for them, nor are you even a thought. They could care less about your well being. If you have never thought of an adult verbal or psychological abuser as being a criminal, perhaps it's time you wake up. Most adults who enjoy abusing the innocent are people with a bad mentality. They are not people I would ever think of as having a conscience. And try as you might, most will never be a candidate for self-improvement. Don't waste your time. Some human beings with bad attitudes are just not reachable by the rest of us. If you are one who craves peace, you will not find it in the company of these individuals. Getting them to realize their wicked ways is a job best left to time. Obviously, what hurts us is not good for us. Start making more of the choices that will enrich your life in all the ways that count with your Creator. Someone decided they were going to trash your life? That's an arrogance you do not have to keep tolerating. Don't allow the toxic mess to keep coming back to you. It is more than shameful to keep helping to trash your own life. It is also wasteful. You are way more intelligent than you have allowed yourself to be. Fueling your mind with toxic memories is a backlash whose privileges should be revoked. If a painful experience must forever change you, let it power you up, not weaken you down. Get serious about your own happiness and give yourself a brand new better welcome to life. You will love it. You cannot afford to let anyone or anything keep you daydreaming in horror. Dedicate your best to you first. Unspeakable joy will follow—you can guarantee that.

MORE AWAKENING TRUTHS

I PRAY that by the conclusion of this message, you will look at yourself in the new way that will make you realize you were not sent to this planet to represent illegal dumping. You don't have to keep carrying the heavy loads of past unfairness or present ones that might be controlling your life. You can take this time in your life to let go of the invading wrongs. Make it your biggest drop. Have faith in the powerful goodness of your own humanity. Building a new life away from the falsehoods provided by mental anguish and low self-esteem is not challenge free, but you do have it within your power to soar above it all. Skipping your own life, in my opinion, would be a terrible waste. The idea that someone else could force you to should be unacceptable to you. I have not doubt that no matter how wracked with pain you are, you do realize that living in an institution of pain and living a freedom filled joyful life are two separate things. You can not be living in an uncomfortable place and tell yourself you're free. That's an awful waste of precious time. Your life is meant to be a beautiful presentation. As long as you are still breathing, it's not too late to start seeing yourself as the valuable person that you are. You should not be numb as your life is happening. You should be fully present, fully alert, fully in charge. Charging yourself for a crime you did not commit is not only foolish, but it's robbing your soul of its powerful light. Turning on yourself in such an unfair way will most certainly keep you from shining as brightly as you should. You need more than the past needs. You—your one and only life in the flesh should not be guided by endless flashbacks of horrors. The enormous amounts of mental energy spent doing so is sinful. The pressure on your life from this exhausting distraction is careless company.

It's a cruel distraction you can live better without. There are millions of misguided souls on our planet who use and abuse themselves in one form or another everyday, yet I can guarantee you that not one of these lost souls will get to the end of their lives thanking themselves with a pat on the back for having the presence of mind to throw away their remaining days to self inflicted wounds. No sane human being will ever declare that sadness feels good. Sadness should be avoided as though it were a plague. For me, the years I allowed sadness to re-arrange my life had enormous and far reaching consequences. Living with constant sadness is a price no innocent human being can afford to keep paying. Pain is something that causes our lives to loose volume, no matter what kind of pain it is that you have or are experiencing. It's just not something most sane people want in their lives. Sadness is a pain you have the strength to fight and win. The very fact that sadness is the wrong kind of life to live should make you all the more determined to free your mind. Your body will reward you in amazing ways. Don't let a life of sadness be as good as it gets for you. Get as good as you can get. Live your life as good as is possible. Years of relentless sadness in the life of any victim of cruel circumstances is a life arrested too long. Why wait for your time in sadness to bring you more suffering before you decide your suffering has been long enough? At this point in my life after surviving so many of life's unexpected cruelties, I would not think of dealing with pain without my positive power present. There is certainly no longer any room in my mind for bad memories to fit comfortably, nor is there any room in my life for bad people. Unleashing unpleasantness into ones own life should always be forbidden. Embracing all that is good for your mind, body and soul is the better hold. Holding on to sadness and making it a part of every important decision you make for yourself will continue to make you less whole. You can make wiser choices by removing sadness from the center of your life. As your mental health improves, so will the quality of your life for sure. Celebrating your life means miracles will be easier to come by. Happiness is your real life. It's what will make your life as high as you can see. You will find a daily supply of laughter extremely valuable. A season of grief should not run the entire length of your life. Its tormenting takes an enormous toll on every area of your life, including those people still in denial, still conducting daily remembrance tours harmful to their minds. For many of these people, restoration has never been attempted. They are still living engulfed by an inferno of emotional pain. No one has ever paid less for a painful past by holding onto it. Just try to imagine how high the price will be if you decide to hold onto it until it becomes antique. Hopefully I got a smile out of you. I am sure you will agree there are too many of our fellow human beings who are constantly searching for new ways to be more destructive. Don't join in by denying yourself peace. Keep the best of you as alive as you should be. Inner peace is something you can get nowhere else. The tormenting spirit of evil doers is not a legacy to be preserved in you. Using a wiser faith-filled attitude will make it easier to stamp out the flames your mind's resources should not be wasted on, that which will never be to your benefit. Use your powerful mind to discover the genius in you. Become mentally healthy-wealthy. A positive attitude is your best clean up effort. Why not enhance the good life experiences that you can? Everything as we know it will eventually come to an end, including the sadness that so many people are still willing to live with foolishly waiting for the hands of time to release them from its grip. When it comes to your inner peace, acting in haste is must. There is not a wasteful minute of your life to spare on anything less. You are greatness not to be wasted. You have no responsibility to sadness. Never fail to remind yourself that time is faster than any human being. Hurry up and live in a high level of joy. Take your place in a wiser peacefulness and prosper as you should. You know as I do that our presence here on earth will never force time to stand still. Why not make the best of your stay? Start giving yourself mega doses of joy. Who deserves joy more than the innocent suffering souls?

A wiser living now is a choice you should be able to make in one breath. Obviously, the same mind that can become so preoccupied with tormenting memories is also your protection against the evils that are blocking your blessings. Never face another day without reminding yourself you can change your thinking to a much happier you. God truly does reward those who are willing to help themselves. The most positive building steps must be taken by you. God does respond to a willing good heart. There is no love in the mistreatment of your mind, no matter who is doing it to you, a thoughtless cruel abusive deviant or you yourself. Your love for yourself should be as unconditional as you wish others to love you always. Now that you are mature enough to protect your soul to the best of your ability, emotional anguish should not continue to define your life. Endlessly short changing yourself will never give the true balance to your life that you need. The victimization of self is such a nasty negative. It's what I call the bad bonus. Having a self-defeating mentality, regardless of abuse suffered, is a mentality that is the worst of enemies. For your protection, you need a powerful positive new direction. If you decided today to stop denying yourself the kind of strength and courage you need to offer yourself the right kind of unconditional love, it will grow in heavenly leaps and bounds around you so beautifully and so wide you will not be able to skip anymore of your life. While you have breath, supply yourself with the greatness that is far better for you than bitterness. Use the experience of any ugly injustice applied to your life as the great lesson that can lead you to new spiritual growth and a more powerfully correct life. I realize from my own childhood experience that for most helpless victims of abuse, there is an environment of fear that weakens and robs confidence. It's an ungodly environment that changes some lives in dangerous ways, self-hatred being the most dangerous. Abuse verbal or physical forces the victims to make negative self adjustments whether the victims is aware they are making these adjustments or not. The sins of others should not be allowed to blight your remaining days. Someone more powerful than you were at the time violated your human rights, inflicted what no soul or mind should be forced to bear, and left you to journey through life living the lies you were told about your value as a human being. It left you feeling as if you lack survival skills, as if you are not important, not good enough, not worthy of respect, not worthy of true lasting love and a joy-filled journey. Don't believe the lies that you will never be able to do better. One of your first factual reminders should always be to never forget that what abusers of the innocent hope to accomplish is to make you feel less human, less valuable, and as a result, end up hating yourself as much as they hate themselves. It's the misery-loves-company go round in the most painfully dizzying of ways. No one who understands the power of love could use anything less. Abuse, physical or emotional, is not love. It has nothing to do with love. It's about using the power of evil to control another human being. Abuse, whether it is emotional, physical, mental, or whatever the case might be, is the planting of negative seeds in the victim's mind, seeds fertilized by the emotional pain it causes. Even so, you don't have to let those seeds continue growing in you. No matter how well rooted those negative seeds are. It is still possible to take your life back from the disgusting evil system that was forced upon you. At the same time, I also realize that not every victim of abuse can have or want a quick end to their sorrow. Some people have gotten to the point where they no longer care that they are soaking themselves in bitterness every breath. Living in a state of constant sadness is a bondage no one should let themselves become accustomed to. It should never feel like a natural part of your humanity, depression, sadness, inner conflicts, all sources of difficulties. It is impossible to find a good balance for your life when all of this is going on in a mind that was created for joy. It is a surrender to the domination of past evils. Your abuser should never be allowed to influence the rest of your life. Bad influences are offensive instruments no matter how privately or quietly they were applied to your life. When someone tells you that you are ugly, worthless, and useless, that you are not good for anything, that you will never come off to anything good in this world, and on and on they go, what they are actually doing is describing to you how they feel about themselves. You are seen by this kind of abuser as a place to drop their dangerous toxins. Don't hold it for them. Don't help anyone carry their mind garbage. If they loved you, they would not have forced it on you. Don't let them continue helping themselves to your life. You did not come into this world with a subscription to garbage. You did not subscribe to it, so why hand over the rest of your days to abuse of any kind? Let yourself be as free as God's wishes. Don't continue to follow the map that was designed for your life by someone with a muck-filled mind. You were not created to be in intensely painful conflicts with yourself. I had to learn through painful consequences that having a good relationship with myself must be first priority. Making and maintaining a peaceful relationship with yourself is very necessary to keep the effects of abuse from reducing your life in all the wrong ways. That's the reality! It is also a reality that God gave you an amazing mind not meant to cause you daily grief. Having an adult life beset by childhood emotional difficulties when you could prevent those memories from demanding you is a waste of precious life, especially if you are one of those unfortunate souls that have stuck unfair negative labels on yourself. Compromising your safety in any way, shape or form is not a way to make miracles happen. The miracles in store that you need will come to you through faith and a permanent positive attitude. We get what we pray for more often than we realize. A permanent positive attitude is a miracle-filled prayer in progress. Start praying and make sure you stay tuned. A brand new positive attitude will move your life forward, but you must be willing to change any unfair negative opinion that you may have of yourself. From the moment you became a thought in the mind of God, much was prepared for you, none of which includes bad obsessions. Negative remembrances being used to inflict new pain on yourself will never give you a great future, not ever. Someone else's selfishness should not continue to dominate your life. Losing your God-given connection with yourself is an unaffordable loss. Why share your abuser's fate when you don't have to? Why not be the champion of your own life? You do deserve more than a dinky little life. You need no one's approval to stick up for yourself and let your powerful spirit shine. Somewhere deep in your soul, you must know that a life of unpleasantness is not the Divine's intended purpose for your life. You are special. You are important. You are valuable in every possible sense. Don't allow anything or anyone to keep directing your life towards the trash can. No one here on earth should get your permission to spoil your chances of having a God-great life. The abuse of your being is the worst kind of insult, no matter who is doing it. No part of your life should be that tough. This kind of abuse is way more than bad manners. It is the breaking down of your power base. Without your good mental health you cannot be as powerful in your own life as you should be. You were not created to be a brave source of sick evil entertainment. Everything in your power should be done to keep yourself from becoming one of those poor innocent souls who realized too late they took too long to live their best life and lost so much valuable time. There are so many adult victims of abuse who has yet to realize that they were used by their abuser to help represent unpleasantness, to spread it around like a virus. As difficult as that is to hear, it's the kind of truth you must face if you are to heal up in order to power yourself up. Make it no longer necessary to ignore the beauty of your own life. A life that is experiencing abuse in any form is a life in captivity. There are adults who are able to leave an abusive situation yet feels that they have no choice but to accept the miserable condition that they are in. I still believe our own negative misguided thoughts and beliefs are far more damaging to us more often than we realize. You don't need anyone to bring you perfect timing. Low self esteem is a practice you yourself can stop. Your life is a very big deal. It's time you see it as such. You are not supposed to think of yourself as anything less than the great power that you were created from. As an adult you have a responsibility to protect your own life and preserve your sanity. Every human being should refuse to accept a negative shift in the quality of their lives. Purposefully eliminating yourself from a peaceful joyful life in order to make yourself available for the abusive convenience of others is not only cruel, it's the bottom of the pit low self-esteem which also means you are in a desperate semifinal situation. For your own safety, get out of this insane mentality before someone else with no respect for the precious gift of life decides for you how your life should be finalized. It takes only an ounce of common sense to get you started on the process of updating your life to a safer environment. Do it before there is not enough of your humanity left to do it with. Everyday that an innocent human being remains in an environment of abuse is a day that lessens that victim in the worst of ways. Every act of abuse that you accept pushes you further away from your truest self. No matter how many generations of people in your family before you that accept being abused as the norm, it is time for you to stop living in accordance with this horrible tradition. The abuse of another human being is unacceptable behavior. This kind of bad behavior comes from people with a corrupt mentality. There are rotten people with their self defeating mentality living and walking among us desperately seeking to recruit. Defend your life! Yes you can. You have the inner strength to remove yourself from the self defeating mentality of others. It has been proven billions of times that some of our fellow human beings cannot be trusted to care for the life of another as if it were their own. Nevertheless, this unfortunate fact should not keep you from trusting in the one everlasting Power that is responsible for giving you life. Life is a tremendous opportunity. Please don't throw yours away. I wish you could see yourself through the eyes of God. Perhaps then you would realize how truly precious you are and start doing more of the good things you need to do to be an even wiser survivor. What you should always keep in mind is the fact that you did not choose you. You had nothing to do with your entrance into this world. Your creation was the decision of the greatest power that there is. Don't live ignorant of your value as a human being. Allowing yourself to be mistreated is to give the servants of evil permission to criticize God's choice. Who created for you a destiny of ill treatments and to be misunderstood? I can assure you God is not responsible for creating any such destiny. God created a lot of things, yet I can tell you with certainty that bad destinies were not included. If you remove your life from the bad destiny others have planned for you make no mistake about it. You will be fully understood, and that in spite of any oppositions. For now and always, to thine own self be truer. Yours is a life that truly matters. That is the reason you were created as beautiful as the dawn, you are so precious that guardian angel awaited and welcomed your arrival. You came from a kingdom of great purpose. God earned your trust by creating you from the power of unconditional love. You owe it to yourself and to the Creator of your life to live wisely. Your life should not be kicked along or left to tumble like weeds in the desert dust. You can escape the traps of cruel interferences and live your full beautiful life. Use the power of faith as you would a protective muscle. You will achieve the peaceful desires of your heart. All that you were meant to be is written in victory. If you are willing to do your part, faith will take you to the miraculous places you were meant to be. There are countless sweet joyful experiences waiting for your permission to be delivered, further proof you were born worthy. You are more than good enough for blessings. You were not a speedy last minute fit. You were given the gift of life to love and cherish you first. You are a very important part of reality. Appreciating the gift of your own life will keep you from stagnant complacency. You are the greatest value that was added to days. Become a wiser user of them. Your life will go further, but you must stop accepting a poor quality of life as the norm. Before we were even given the gift of life, our days were measured. Why waste the best gift you were ever blessed with? There will never be enough of it to be wasted. Refuse to be held back. You arrived into the world with a clean life. Don't allow someone else's muck to cover and keep mudding up your life. You were also given the gift of positiveness in every breath. Live unafraid. Why live in fear of being abused when you don't have to? Live bravely in your own life. Why allow past or present abuse to keep you under its toxic spell? Your life should not be lived to please the people who believe they have more power over your life than the Creator of life. Make it clear to every destructive force that your life is not for anyone or anything to destroy. No self respecting, sane able body adult should ever live their life at the mercy of an abuser. Every living thing that is created from the power of divine love was also created to be free. Why should you not invest more in your own freedom? You are a priceless treasure who was made to live well. No abuser of the innocent will ever be able to hand anyone a free day. They are instead robbing days of freedom that no one can afford to lose. Your free days were given to you by the Creator of days. No other life here on earth owns your life. Now that you are no longer a child, no one should get to do with your life whatever they please. Why should they have two lives to use while you have none? The things created by God to add more beauty and happiness to daily life belong to you too. Having or accepting less will bring you regrets. Keep in mind there will always be people in the world who will see you as too much of a good thing and try to destroy the positive power within. If given the opportunity, they will nibble down your life. Never give anyone the opportunity to seduce you into their vicious killer cycles. It's not an adjustment you were born to make. Emotional pain is not a structure to hold you together better. It is more like being dragged to the edge of a cliff. Having a difficult childhood should not be used as an excuse to unleash unpleasantness into your adult life. Don't ignore happiness before giving it a try. Now that you are no longer a helpless child, no one should be allowed to strip you of your self esteem. You are entitled to your human dignity. No one should ever be able to convince you that they are more valuable than you are. No human being can decide for the only Creator of life what the ultimate physical beauty should be. The fact that you are the property of the Most High means that there is nothing more beautiful than you. You are not meant to be included in the ugliness that our fellow human being has created. Keep in mind, no human being can create anything that is as beautiful or as perfect as the Creator of all things that have life. It is impossible for any human being to be as knowledgeable as God. Don't let anyone convince you that they have the right to take away your God given right to live a peaceful life of freedom and joy. Every single thing that was created naturally to sustain life came straight from the heart of the wiser of us. Refuse to be convinced by any fellow human being that they were chosen by God to rule your life. A life of full blown ignorance is what you don't need. Our fear and rejection of the best things available to us, such as inner strength, courage and peace, just to name a few, are some of the reasons there are so many tormented souls among us. Souls so tormented the moment they realize how special you are they will hate your for it and zoom in for the kill. Don't let these disgusting experiences sink into you forever. Put these emotional traumas back where they belong. This does not mean lowering yourself to your abuser's level. What I am suggesting is that you refuse to let the bad attitudes of others take over your live. Most abusers are not going to volunteer to stop ruining your life. For most of these deviants being a tormentor is the twisted way they choose to feel human. They don't care that this kind of abusive attitude does not enhance any God given gift that they might have. Give them a double dose of what they hate about you. Be even more awesome in your love and respect of self. Be adventurous. Get to know you better. Be more breathtaking. Have a bright life that is open to newness. This brand new great attitude of yours will hurt them in all the right ways. Don't live your life feeling dirty and low, wasting precious breath calling yourself a nothing. It's not who you are, it's not what you are, it's not how your were made. You are a true heaven-sent being made with powerful survivorship. Embrace your life. Return to your full native heaven-sent self. There is where you will fine much more survivorship. Your seat of power is not for anyone else to sit in. Remind them who is in charge. Take back the earthly controls of your life. You are an important message from God. Hurry to deliver. Celebrate your life in big ways. There is no time to waste. Don't dwell on the provoking lies that you were told about who and what you are. Dwelling on these lies will leave you too tired to concentrate on the things that are best for your mental health. At the same time, I do realize that there are events forced into our memory that are so painful, recalling them can leave us with a feeling of being punched in the gut every time our mind renews them, making it difficult to live without the element of fear that forces the heart to tremble. Nevertheless, you can get out from under the spell of the past. The quiet inner explosions that come from such memories will certainly continue to interfere with your most precious gift—your life. If emotional pain resulting from past experiences is allowed to keep you under its spell, you will never get the most out of the rest of your life. Perhaps you are one who can say to yourself, "Today, I have already survived the worst!" If so, why not give your life the good chance that you deserve? I am asking this of you because I know from first hand experience that abuse of any kind applied to an innocent human being can lead to an enormous loss of self that can take many years to recover. This is especially true for those victims whose painful raw memories are allowed to keep a choke hold on their mental health. This is very much like living with the major fires of hell blazing out of control, a secret inner fire no one else can see or hear, a torture chamber, an internal world of pain. I lived it. That is how I know. That is how I also know that giving permission to the memories of past cruelties to keep you under its spell is a negative with too high a price. The quiet violent inner explosions that are caused by those painful memories will—without a doubt—continue to interfere with all areas of your life. Our life was not given to be spent in painful recollections. It is so much healthier and wiser to let positive thoughts and good memories be the only giants that live in your mind. All of your future predictions for your life should be nothing less than powerfully positive. The human mind is very powerful. Use faith to draw into your life only those things that will bring you happiness. It would be wise to bear in mind that most of the time the unfortunate events that brings us the most pain are not disasters that we could have prepared for, which is another reason why junking the rest of your life to sadness is a terrible waste of life.

Living in the memories of unpleasantness drains the mind of its ability to stay in the present. In order to have your best life living consciously is a must. The cost of being human is sometimes as high as we ourselves place it. Letting your mind live back there in those past bitter days is a merciless bad habit you can live without quite nicely. You need not condemn yourself because of the sins of others. Willfully choosing to continue to include in your daily life emotions that are certain to cause further injuries is a life of sadness no one should embrace. Like every other human being alive on the planet, today you too were given the gift of freewill. Why use this wonderful precious gift to give up on yourself? The gift of free will was not given to you to be used against your own humanity so you could feel hopeless and helpless. This great power was given to human kind to be used as the wise enhancer that it is. Too many of us take for granted the gift of freewill. Why abuse yourself because you possess the power to do so? Every single gift from the most high was divinely thought out—freewill no less so. The power of freewill should always be used as the blessing that it is. Let it serve in your life all of the wonderful purposes that it was intended to. Why not use your God given freewill and the positive power within to contribute happiness to every area of your life? Show your appreciation for all of life's loving gifts. This wonderful attitude will encourage more priceless blessing. Life's greatest rewards should not be inaccessible to you because your sadness is standing in the way keeping you detached from your best living. You were not created second best. Don't let past disappointments and the sadness that results lower your ability to make the choices best for your life. This one and only life that we have should not be wasted, not a single day. Living the rest of your life as thought you are a trapped animal is an added cruelty your soul should not have to endure. No cruelty you have experienced will ever feel sorry for you and one day suddenly decide to hand you back your life as it were before the unfairness came to bear. Yesterday is done. It's forever, but today is yours. Make it your greatest wish come true. Make today the great new opportunity you have been waiting for to do better for yourself. Can you think of a greater opportunity to renew your spirit than the opportunity of this new day that you are blessed to have? Whether it was good or bad, the past will never undo itself no matter how many times or in how many ways you wished it so, making it pointless to waste your time waiting for a reversal. Waiting is wasting!

It is an undisputable fact that intensely painful emotional experiences are most often what are responsible for the major shifts in the direction of our lives. I hope you have already realized that I am not suggesting to you that sorrow is not difficult to deal with. Of course it is. Regardless of which unfortunate event or events it arrived to you, it is difficult to deal or adjust to because you were not created to spend your life suffering. Suffering is not the intended purpose of your life. You were not created to be transported to restlessness. No kind of sad emotion will ever feel right to a healthy mind. Horrible reflections are so toxic and abusive to the entire being. Besides being infuriating, lingering horrible realities with its high level of contaminants can be very diminishing if they are given your permission to be. Being alive is a great thing, but if you are one who is living with sadness, you are certainly not yet living your best life. Living sad is a present danger that often brings unintended consequences. You can live better. Would it be so difficult for you to admit that to yourself? You should be living better. It is your birthright to do so. It can not be soon enough. The way that you live your life must be special because you are special, as in especially good. If the Creator of the universe and all life on earth were not able to fulfill your needs, you would not have been created. You would not be a part of the circle of life. You would not have been created to rely on that power that is above all powers. That is the power with the greatest managing skills. I had to trust in that fact even as the losses piled up in my own life. It is not always easy to trust in what some people see as an invisible power. Nevertheless, I have found it to be the greatest especially because there is no limit to the miracles that are so generously given. You are an investment of the Divine. Make yourself one of the best this world has ever seen. Stop fretting about the tides. Above it is where you were born to rise. You don't have to keep living in years of unrealized dreams, not when you can harvest the positive power in you. Self torture will not change the unchangeable. It will, instead, move your life further away from its rightful course. Nothing that keeps you from fulfilling your true purpose should be encouraged. You are one of the true sources that can be traced back to God. Refuse to be ungrateful to the hands that molded you. In spite of pain and suffering, the one person here on earth that you should never loose faith and trust in is yourself. No matter what cruel circumstance it was or who it was that set an example of self rejection for you, it is not wise to live carelessly by those negative examples that were such a crime against your humanity. Giving into inner chaos is not a way to positive advancement. Trust and love yourself enough to faith your way out of the nightmares that are tormenting your days. It is time to love yourself to freedom. If not now, when? If you are willing to love yourself more, to respect yourself more, I believe you will move the mighty miraculous powers of the heavens and the earth. If you are waiting on someone else's approval or permission to live a life of happiness, you will never be able to fully embrace the miracle of you, or realize all of the wonderful reasons for your existence. Your life is exclusively yours. Don't donate it to more danger. Your precious life is your gift to celebrate and enjoy. You were not built to carry a toxic concentration of pain. I can tell you for a fact that the negative thoughts that come to the mind as a result of the gut busting emotional anguish can cast dark shadows that will hold back your life from every great standard of excellence. No one should ever ignore a big low hanging dark cloud. You do not want to bet your life on its rain. It is no secret that sadness prolonged robs ambition. You should decide that you will not let another day go by before embracing the fact that life should be a positive journey. As you take your breaths, every area of your life should be satisfying instead of the absolute horrors that I can assure you is not a punishment from the loving hands that created you. You should be experiencing the highest level of joy that there is. It is not in the creator's plan for you to suffer. I have proven for myself that an attitude of faith is far more powerful than living one's life looking back on the events that we will never be able to reverse. If we could erase past disappointments along with the people who sometimes are responsible for forcing them into our lives just by remembering those disappointments, the world might be without us. Why not use the natural God-given make up of your mind to power you forward to your better days? Don't be one who realizes too late. You have today. Today is such a beautiful chance. Why not use it to your benefit? You do not have to be a victim for the rest of your days. Your value as a human being did not come from the bottom of the trash can as your abusers told you it did. Your value as a human being came from the One and only original divine Power. You are not one of those man-made things that don't add up. You do add up. You are one of the greatest human beings who ever lived. You came from a power that will never fail, no matter how many times you fail. Jehovah's power will never be lessen, even when it seems the odds are against us. You were created a whole soul, a precious, heavenly seed not meant to be planted in toxic soil. You are not ordinary. You were not created by ordinary hands. You were not created with ordinary power. You were not created from ordinary thoughts, nor were you created in an ordinary way. You came from a great Power that is above all powers. The creative power that you were made from is one that no human being will ever be able to change no matter how many times or in how many ways cruel words from acid tongues are used against you. No one and nothing on this earth can diminish the extraordinary power that created you no matter how many times the enemies wish it to be so. No other human being was ever given the power or the right by God to decide that your value as a human being should be lower than anyone else's. You were not molded from an afterthought. You are not a creation of evil. Evil's ugly words are not what you were formed from. You are the result of a brilliant power that has nothing to do with ordinary. You are what went right. Strong enough is not what you can be, it's what you are. You have power. You have inner strength. Tap into it. Stop living tense. Getting stuck on the things that will never be beneficial to your mental health is careless living. Whatever the unfairness is or was in your life, I have no doubt that God took notice of it. You really do not need to get stuck in a nightmare. Make it history. It may not always seem easy to do, but it can be done. You can live the freedom way that was planned out for your life's journey. The great power you were blessed with is still in you. Don't give worries a permanent place in your life. It is a horrible waste of your life's time. You are a once in a life time opportunity. Why throw yourself into sadness, deep depression, physical abuse, and the emotional and mental anguish that result? I call these the "bad transportation". They need not be transported into you forever. Sometimes in our adult life, we set ourselves up for cruel disappointments without realizing that we were. Now think how unfair it is to you and how foolish it is to use that fact as an excuse to ignore the nourishment that your soul needs to survive at its best. Why would any sane adult person give up their God-given right to have a peaceful, joyful life? Most of us can and should remove our lives from the adversities others are so determined to make a part of our daily lives. Such oncoming disasters with their life threatening toxins should never have your approval, let alone your surrender. Your life is not stamped "BAD DESTINY". No one has the right to put your life on a path of tragic wrongs. When it comes to your life, the avoidable nightmares must be avoided. Other people's garbage does not have to have the power over your life that you think it does or are allowing it to be. Allowing fear to control your life for the benefit and enjoyment of someone with a twisted abusive mentality is a dreadful waste of your life. You were born to be naturally happy and free. Be the freedom that rings the loudest. The very fact that any adult who is able to remove themselves from an abusive environment would refuse to do so is the very reason they will never receive an ounce of true lasting respect from their abuser. What abusive coward is going to give you the respect they don't even have for themselves? Most people who enjoy making trouble for their fellow human beings are most often weak minded people using others to hide behind. These deeply insecure troublemakers may not realize their true purpose in life until they are properly schooled by the pegs of time. The behaviors in others that we should find frightening from the moment we are introduced to them is often the behaviors we ignore by finding every excuse to deny the manipulating tragic realities instead of the fast risk assessment and survival running that we should be doing. If from the first moment that a troublemaker began casually uprooting you from your place of peace, you refused to let them take over your adult life. They would not be able to develop into the high cost that they eventually become. A peaceful place is a powerful place to be in your life. In order for any enemy to control you, they must render you weak. And in order to render you weak, your peace of mind is the first thing that has to be stolen. No matter how angry or how disappointed you are feeling about the cruel events that were beyond your control, know that God is still in control. It matters not where we reside on this planet of God's or who we are. If we are aware of this ultimate decider some of us call God, then I am certain that most believers have found cause at one time or another to get angry with God, or at the very least ask in anger, "Why?" Nevertheless, God loves us. That is a fact that will not change even when we ourselves refuse to change for the better. God gives us love willingly and generously. God's love and grace is all around us. Every beautiful thing on this face of the earth that you must have to survive was created in anticipation of you. Your life starting with your greatest of grandparents that lived and walked the earth thousands of years ago can be traced back to the most resourceful divinely powerful Almighty. God's time leads up to you. When He was ready, you the lovely lead up were given your life. Is it any wonder then that He has an enormous interest in your life starting long before your great new beginning in the womb was realized? Now it is time for you to realize your own power as a human being with divine purpose. Since you are not a remote control robot, you should not allow yourself to be treated as such. You are very significant, whether you see yourself that way or not. Don't be convinced that you are less than significant. You are not a possibility. You are a living, breathing, beautiful reality that came from a still loving, living power. The light of God is still shining on your life. Choose today to be the day that you strengthen your resolve and follow the course charted for you by your Creator. Today, like all of the other days that we have survived, is a day that we are blessed to have the opportunity that is the great gift of life. Today we can enjoy the pleasure of a lovely gentle breeze. Feel the warmth of the sun. Perhaps listen with a smile in our hearts to a few beautiful bird songs, or to the sounds of water rushing along in its natural nature places. Each and every one of us owes it to our Creator to make the most of each and everyday that we are blessed to be alive, instead of living your life on the pile of dreadful ruin that criminals demand that you do. There is no reason why your good mind should be disfigured and become flimsy because you had the misfortune of encountering a disturbing violently abusive deviant. No one can dispute the fact that there is injustice in the world. There are unimaginable crimes going on all around the world every moment of every day. We cannot blame God for any of these crimes. We have only ourselves as human beings to blame for our wickedness to each other. In many ways, I see us as God's best results. Unfortunately, not enough of us humans see ourselves that way. Perhaps if more people did, we would not have the environments of antagonism that we do. Life was not given to us to become a heavy burden. Life was not given as a curse to the receiver. That was not the intended effect. A life of comfort and joy at its highest level is the advance arrangement that was made for you. Extreme uneasiness should not be managing your life. You should not be living spiritually destitute. Such a state will only enlarge any problem that you might have. The wonderful extraordinary intention of God was for you to grow up with and use the same power that was used to form you. When your soul entered into that bran new phase of flesh and blood, that particular reconstruction of your soul was not meant to exist without the use and benefit of the great power that your were created from. I really believe the reason suffering is so described is because it is truly uncharacteristic of our humanity. There was a time in my life when because of my own suffering I was convinced some of us were born to suffer. Why else would we encounter such difficulties, finding ourselves in our most innocent of years being taken advantage of in some of the most cruel indecent of ways? When God created life, bad behavior was not one of the things that were brought together in our humanity by such positive hands. People who are bad are that way because they choose to be. I am no longer of the mentality some of us were born into the world for the sole purpose of suffering. I will never resort to such negative beliefs again. No one can afford to risk being weakened by such thoughts. Most of the adults who still believe that they were born to suffer are often people who have accepted the negative narrow-minded predictions of careless thoughtless tongues that were made for their lives long ago. Without even realizing it, they had accepted such negative predictions that keep laying down the wrong kinds of foundation. Choosing to live with the belief that your only reason for existing on this earth is to suffer is not a direction anyone should be pointing their life in. We should always be willing to look for ways to maintain our spiritual strength instead of becoming a danger to ourselves. "I was born to suffer," are the words that should never come together in your heart, let along on your tongue. Defy cruelty. Go to music school instead of allowing toxic beliefs to take over your mind and your life. Become as you were meant to be, the highest light of your life. Include yourself in the joy-filled, meaningful, purpose-filled places that you belong. Loving and appreciating your own life should not be a difficult task. Ignoring your own health will not lead to the demise of every bad person alive today. There are people that are living so frustrated they cannot see beyond the emotional pain long enough to want to protect their own lives. Heavy burdens with their detrimental effects that can be tossed aside should be, in its place, should be the best powerfully positive difference that is the Almighty Savior. In spite of the terrible disappointments that we sometimes have to face having the breath of life is still an enormous blessing that we should be grateful to have. The world is not always going to be kind to you, but you can always be kind to yourself. You should never live the examples set for you by the murderous offensive. The examples of anger, rage, and bitterness are always brought into one's self without fully understanding the accompanying risks. The bad mood that is a constant companion of these emotions even when deeply hidden can be for some people as deadly as the predators of fellow human beings. Purify as you survive. You are stronger than the expectations of evil. Why not have these bad stimulants abolished? You don't need the recklessness that anger, rage, and bitterness can sometimes inspire. Difficulty coping will become less and less of a challenge after you accept that you do deserved to be happy. Smarter choices are ours to make whenever possible. Isn't it wonderful that you don't need to put in an application for approval from any other human being to reach your most remarkable level of excellence? You are no exception to God's rules and desire for happiness for every living thing that was created by His hands. You are a natural part of the tradition of God's. You should not be forced by anyone from Satan's work force to pay dearly for your existence. A majestic unlimited amount of love is yours from the Almighty. Make that fact count! After all it's how your life was perfected. Luckily for us, we do not have to leave our earthly home to receive and benefit from this love. Our souls and spirit can be nourished daily if we are willing to embrace peace as we cast our focus on the very best that faith itself has to offer us. Faith is far bigger, far more powerful than any cruelty that you have ever experienced in your life. Living without fear to faith will make it so much easier to embrace the God-given power within. Your life can go a lot better than any tormenting difficulties, especially if you are one that can acknowledge that God is on your side. If you can, you will soon realize that even in the times when it seems that you have lost, you will never lose a battle. Hold onto your peace. Let God fight your battles for you. No one does it better. This is not to suggest you turn any cheek. You are no one's door mat. There is no person standing out on the sidewalk somewhere giving out free breath, telling you to "come on, step right up and take a breath. It's free." Every free breath that we are given comes to us as a precious gift from our Creator. No one is given or will ever be given permission from God to door mat you. Wasting years of your life now will leave you dying to get those wasted years back. Time from your life is not something you should allow any one to steal, not if you can help it. It is important for all of us to recognize how important our mental and emotional health is regardless of age. If you want to look and feel your best, positive emotions should always be flowing through you. Don't put off your happiness. It is the one thing that should not be on your waiting list. Be more conscious of your spiritual needs. You will profit greatly. This wonderful consciousness will lead to your happiness. Living with a troubled mind and the instability that often results is a sure way to cut your life short. Thankfully, because of the gift of freewill, we can choose to live as peaceful as a river. Having faith in God means that what's yet to come is nothing less than the best victories. Mega doses of strengthening benefits are yours to harvest by faith. It is always far more beneficial to follow the one and only true Divine Guidance than to continue giving yourself permission to get trampled on by the parade of pain-laced days that are sure to steal more precious years from your life. Unfairness does not have to destroy your true character, nor does it have to destroy the rest of your life. Shutting down the best of who you are in order to donate more of your time to unpleasant memories is truly unwise. Your spiritual welfare should always be of great concern to you. It is difficult to gain real benefit from a life in turmoil. The truth is, here on earth as we life and move among our fellow human beings, there is no guaranteed security system in place against the tormenting demonic spirit of tyrants. That is how they choose to use their gift of freewill. Unfortunately, there are too many restless souls in the world today. Refuse to be one of them. Keep in mind that a never ending cycle of personal mental anguish has nothing to do with self-respect and love of self. You don't torture what you love. Living backwards in mental anguish could be described as banishing yourself from life. Sadness is such a lonely place to live. The gift of life (most definitely including your own), should be honored with all things positive. Sadness allowed to linger for years is very much like locking yourself in a lab where experiments are being conducted daily on willing human guinea pigs, the kinds of experiments that are sure to give bad results. That is just much too rough. It is so much safer to live your life in ways that are wise and so wonderful years from now you won't have to look back on time passed and wish you had taken the necessary actions that would have corrected the problems that are not a part of a healthy lifestyle. Problems given your permission to hang with you will only become stronger and hotter. Even in today's world where more and more are realizing the positive powers and miracles that can and has happened as the result of sincere prayers, there are still people who believe it is better to deal with inner turmoil in inadvisable, unhealthy ways. Some people are convinced that tucking themselves away from the rest of the world with their deep emotional problems will keep them safe from what can become for some its deadly reach. This should not be the case. No kind of emotional problem should ever be given permission to take that much of anyone away. After the passage of time takes us to where we can be described as adults, we should at least try to make positive contributions, starting with our own lives, no matter how small those contributions might be. Please keep the following positive thought in mind as well. Sometimes small can add up to big, dramatic miracles. Why not have faith in the Almighty? This power to live with will be generous to you. Included in our choosing should be to turn over to the Almighty the problems that are just too much for us to bear alone. Whatever you are wise enough to turn over in faith to God will be turned right. Blessings are guaranteed. You can become the gold destination for miracles and end up fitting even more beautifully into life. May I suggest a message of love and unity from you for your soul? This is another kind of positive attitude that will help you to dismiss the deception that could become a threat to the authority God gave you over your own life here on earth, the authority to exercise the faith that will move your life to the higher places that the Almighty has already approved. Why deny yourself a life of sweet successes? It was, after all, positive powers that were intended for our life long use. Negative energy is not a natural part of our humanity. Negative energy is such a destructive force. We should refuse to be a part of it whenever possible. The very fact that it is not a natural part of our humanity is why we should never allow ourselves to be fooled by it. I can guarantee you that the carriers of negative energy will never be rewarded for it heavenly. Some of the most unpleasant human beings that we have the misfortune of encountering are people that are living with the full fury of whatever the problem is that they are not dealing with the right way and is just not interested in recalling a harmful past calmly because they feel there is no reason to hope for better tomorrows. Faith in one's life will leave you with hope to spare. You will never be out of positiveness. Your spirit will be uplifted. The natural God's goodness in this life is not for others alone. It is for you too. Anyone who is willing to give the positive powers of prayer a try can break free from a tormenting past to live a life that is as free as the spirit of our living God. It is truly up to you to choose the best and only lasting way out. Too many of our fellow human beings the world over is dying too soon because of their devotion to sadness. Unrealistic desires are always punishing. Some people who are suffering in sadness are suffering because of their desire to turn back time. I have learned through horrible difficulties that it is always best to accept the reality that it is impossible to return to yesteryears to change the unchangeable. Time will never stand still no matter how determined we are to do so. We are charged with our lives for every second that goes by. What are you using for good? Regardless of who the deceitful, evil manipulator or other unexpected cruelties were that made you live through hell, if you were to choose God for good, the gifts awaiting your reawakening are enough to outnumber the stars in the heavens. From this day forward, be even more blessed. Accept nothing less. No one on the outside of your mind can do for you what you can do for yourself starting right now. A much gentler kinder life can be yours. It is up to you. Why keep revictimizing yourself because other cruelties are demanding that you do? You should not be sacrificing the rest of your life because a cruel event you did not invite was not respecter of you. As you journey through the years, besides the Creator of us human beings, you are the only one here on earth that can respect you best and should do so in spite of any painful disappointments that came to you. It is not necessary to endure bad experiences forever. No one living or in spirit on the other side has the power to use ugly abusive words to minimize or devalue you. It is truly up to you to decide whether or not you want to spend the rest of your life living with the burden of such dangerous trash. Hope should be restored and renewed in all of God's children when we remember that even the tiniest of insects were created with a loving divine purpose. Just think, if those tiny little insects were created to make such positive contribution to this great big planet, can you imagine how precious and how valuable we are too? It is an undisputed fact that as human beings we have yet to realize and use the full resources of our brain, a simpler way to say that is, we have much brain we have yet to use. Wouldn't it be wonderful if everyone who is old enough to see how quickly time moves away from us could also see themselves as the further evidence of miracles that we all are? Unfortunately the reality is that scattered across the globe are otherwise good decent fellow human beings who are living to hate themselves using any number of excuses to do so. I don't believe this would be the case if self haters realize how close by a better way of doing life is. Loving one's self is as close as the human heart. The inner strength needed for a more joyful life is within all of us. My faith in the power that is far greater than human flesh is why I believe that anyone can be removed from emotional bondage no matter how long they have been lying to themselves. You can escape permanently. You have my word on that. There are still millions of people all over the world today who don't realize that the smallest of disappointments does not have to tear their lives apart. Too many times in our lives when we experience disappointments, we fail to see that God is still in control. The same powerful, Almighty God that always has a greater plan for us, the King of the universe is the greatest Fixer-upper that there is. The horrible disappointments in our fellow human beings that leaves us so angry, some of us wonder if God really does love us. It's not the desire of God. God does not want you to suffer. It is never God's wish for any of us to suffer at the hands of His other children. God does not want any of us to live in misery. God's wishes for us do not include suffering. Among His wishes for us is that we prosper and be in good health (3 John 2). This includes your mental and emotional health as well. It is not God's will for us to suffer any wickedness. You can rest assured of that. We also live in a world with bad people included. If we shared a world that only included the good people, most of the tears we shed would be tears of joy. When it comes to God's problem-solving abilities and our own ability to use the positive power in us, the seeds of doubt should never come to bear. We share nothing in common with the seeds of doubt. It's true, in spite of the fact that we allow it to grow on us so often. We all do it, even though we know it is a negative force that, if allowed to, can pull us down. Doubting that God loves you, doubting that you can rise to the level of great success in your finances, doubting that you will ever find that special someone to share your life with, all of these self-doubts and lack of complete faith in the greatest, problem-solving Master is sometimes the result of deep emotional trauma. Unhealthy deposits into the human soul often leave us doubting our own God-given abilities, an unfortunate experience shared by too many of our fellow human beings. Sadness should never stay with you long enough to unravel you. There are many happy ways for you to unravel it instead. Accepting any kind of self-destruction as a part of who you were meant to be is totally wrong. Living sad can quickly become a disease in the human heart. Living sad has no value. It is not worth the extra problems that result. Sadness has a wide range of developments, none of which are good. Living a life of sadness is such a wasteful use of your mind's power. Actually turning one's self into a prisoner of emotional hardship is sure to bring regrets. The hard labor of sadness will never pay off in the right ways. Your good health is the most worthwhile pursuit of happiness that God Himself approves. Perhaps as you read this, you are in that deep sadness place where I used to be, still not loving life as you should, still taking the opportunity of each new day for granted, still not being alive in the joyful way that you should be. What we don't acknowledge can have tragic consequences. That is the reality I was forced by the hands of time to face. Any God-fearing, innocent person having to live with the memories of nightmares that were created for them is a price more than high enough. Allowing those nightmares the power to sleep walk you through your own life is obviously not the way to live your best life. If downhill there were a playground where you could live happier days, I would suggest you keep going downhill. But I know from first hand experience that there is nothing progressive about giving up on yourself. No matter how horrible the difficulties were that we suffered, life goes on. We cannot afford to be intimidated by cruel circumstances for the rest of our lives. Deep sadness left to fester is very much like free falling from a fourteen story building. Sacrificing yourself because of the sins of others is in itself a great sin, not only because you are in danger of being left, not knowing who you really are anymore, but because no one should ever allow their lives to be directed by someone else's toxic destructive rules. No other human being is better than you are. No other human being is more valuable than you are. No other human being is more powerful than you are. They might seem that way to you because perhaps they were given the right opportunities that helped them to realize most of their potentials, but if they can reach for stars, so can you. You don't have to live with a self-defeating mentality. No one on this earth can take God's love away from you. You have the power right there in your mind to put an end to the madness of sadness. Come on out of the darkness. The path to a peaceful life is in your willing hands. When you are willing to give God a chance, God will give you your best chance at freedom from bondage. Living sad is not your best must have self—as in, must have a life that includes the God-given freedom you were sent into the world with, the freedom to have peace. When others look at the life that you are living now it should not remind them of a roller coaster. I know the hellish consequences of being jerked around by an emotional roller coaster life. It's sickening in more ways than many live to count. Thank goodness not everyone whose life has been touched by tragedy finds it difficult to move on, but for those who do, there is a way out of that difficulty. Extremely troubling times do not have to become a permanent part of your existence. Refuse the private lessons so easily given by the seeds of doubt. The seeds of doubt will not help you to grow in the right directions. Harvesting the positive God-given power in you means that you will never be permanently over-powered by any negative force. You will be able to move out of the uninvited fires of hell that were forces upon your life long before it can get the opportunity to drag you to its hottest point of no return. You are a very important part of God's kingdom. If it were not so, none of God's effort and time would have been placed in your creation. If, to date, you are still finding it difficult to believe in you, at least believe that the power that gave you life did so for reasons that are of pure love. There is no limit to the degree in which you can rise above all things negative. It is from that uplifting place that so much will become clearer to you. The successes you can achieve are far beyond anything that you can imagine. You are not only in God's thoughts you are a thought of God's. Don't make yourself into one of those fools who are left starving and thirsting for the impossible reversal of time when you could be drinking in the sweetness of each new day. It is time to stop beating your heart with sorrow. Instead, start living a life that will show the entire world what it means to have courage. Yes, you can. You can do it. You still have life. Finding the courage you need is very possible. Doubting what's possible is a waste of strength no mind can afford. You are as powerful as your freedom to breathe. Use your power to show those who don't know how to get on the right tracks and gift themselves with all of the wonderful things approved by the Creator of life. With faith and healing peacefulness, you will be able to achieve the things you once thought impossible. Let thinking poorly be over and done with. This is a new day. Take fair advantage of the opportunity of being alive and start doing more powerful things with your life. The highest authority wants only the best for you. There is no power in the entire universe that is above that of God's. And if God wants the very best for you, why settle for anything less? You can have a life rich with happiness, starting today, and you don't have to beg for love from anyone. Always remember that no one can love you better. Love yourself enough to acknowledge and embrace that truth. You will be better for doing so, I assure you. Have you ever met someone who has a bad spirit for the first time and only moments after meeting them you cannot only feel their bad spirit in every word they speak but also see it on their entire being? The unpleasantness in which their soul is forced to reside makes you—if only for a moment—wish you were elsewhere. Do whatever good thing it takes to keep you from becoming one of these unpleasant souls. A sad attitude is only inviting to more of the same. I must tell you that whenever I encounter one of these bad spirits, I keep their unpleasantness at a safe distance from my own soul using quiet inner calming prayers and thanks to my Creator for releasing me from the enormous emotional bondage that I was placed in during my childhood by the misguided. Of course because I grow wiser everyday, I don't wait to encounter someone with a bad spirit to be grateful that I finally found the positive power I was created with and is no longer in a long-term relationship with the painful events of my childhood days that created such inner turmoil. On those rare occasions when I think back on how it was, I no longer put my life on the line with those memories. I have become so much stronger than they were a wonderful blessing that I continue to wear joyfully even on cloudy days. I will always be celebrating my restoration. For as long as God allow me to live, I shall keep doing lovely things for myself every single day to celebrate my survival and revival. I will never again put emotional pain first before my health and my life. There is a wealth of God to gain. Live beautifully. Let me tell you now then that even in the worst of memories, I am no longer at the mercy of my attackers. I am no longer disempowered, no longer living in a climate of intimidation and fear. Those cruel memories suffered a permanent setback. I have discovered the strong foundation that was built into me. Another thing that is important to point out is that preventing my abuse would have been the best thing to have happened. In my case, as in the case of too many other innocent little children, still to this day all around the world, I was in an environment of stifling human ignorance. The confusion I experienced was massive fear, physical abuse, and emotional abuse. All of these behaviors were a part of my environment. I feel blessed to have survived not only the initial abuse, but the years following that I sacrificed living my life directed by the horrible sins of others. Please be in agreement with God for your precious life. Please love and embrace the one and only life that you have. Your life is so very important. Please don't waste it. Love the great gift of life that you were given. Take the time to appreciate every breath. Acknowledge that you were created as one of God's best. Love every breath that you take with all of your heart as you love the Lord your God who is bigger and wiser than you and I can think, greater than the heavens and the earth. Isn't it wonderful to know that there is not a single positive thing that you can imagine for yourself that is too big for God to bless you with? Isn't it great to know that God is a power with no impossibilities? If you doubt that, just look in the mirror. You were blessed with life, weren't you? We don't always receive from God in the exact ways in which we had prayed for it to be. Nevertheless, the ways of Almighty God is always the right turn. God is able to turn the worst of your life into the best of your life. God is able to give your life the most spectacular newness. No creation of God can outthink Him, but you can use your mind the way that it was created to be used. Think positively big. Do it everyday. I guarantee your dreaming mind will be a lot more peaceful from now on. Use the positive powers of your mind to erase the night terrors that bad recollections can bring to you. Using your minds positive power will help you to take out the trash. Don't allow cruel events to take over your mind. Stay in good mental health. Want for yourself all of the good things that God wants for you. Give yourself the peace that your soul desires so that you can grow into a better life. The power of God is that even in the ashes is what guarantees your rising. You can bounce back. Remember that in the hands of God, emotional survival rate is a hundred percent, but you must want to survive. God helps those who help themselves. This is a fact I proved for myself. You can make faith work for you as well as it had worked for others. You are entitled to the best. A big share of the inheritance is yours too. Use your freewill to stop the damaging effects of sadness and watch the most beautiful transformation of your life. Challenge yourself with faith. Faith carries a positive power that will reward your efforts. After each human error, no matter how little you might think of yourself, how many times you apply ugly name to your own humanity to put yourself down, you were not created a loser. Neither were you sent in to the world a loser. God does not create losers. Your life was not given to be pushed in the wrong direction. At the very moment of your conception, you were given a positive power so that when you were able to you could use that God-given positive power to steer your life away from the perishing effects of life's cruelties. Our heavenly Father does not oppress; He blesses. What remains of your life can be and should be the best of your life. Why give the rest of your life to a vicious cycle of abuse? The necessary courage needed to remove yourself from this vicious cycle was built into you. You have it, use it. Moses isn't the only one that God gave power to. Finding faith, using faith, finding love and confidence in yourself does not have to be as challenging as you think. God gave you great power tools—use them. Harvest the built-in ambition necessary to keep an active interest in your own life. You should not have to live the rest of your life clinging to the memories of past disappointments. The harvesting of the positive power in you will take your life back to God's choices of fulfillment. Consider the more peaceful life that is God's desire for you an emergency and start living your life with urgency. Life can be very unpredictable. That is something some of us know all too well. There are severe situations that can leave some people wondering if God ran out of mercy before they could call on Him. Let me assure you once more that His mercies will endure forever. As human beings, we may never be able to answer all of the questions we have about the unfairness we sometimes experience in our lives. In the meantime, being honest with ourselves is very important if we are to move on to a better way of surviving. Since we don't get to live in the flesh forever, why not enjoy the life that you have now? Time just keeps slipping away from us. Life cannot be enjoyed fully by anyone who keeps reverting to the anger, rage and bitterness caused by the unfairness that is beyond our own understanding. In the times when we are able, we should deliver ourselves from evil. We know that every life upon the earth today has an expiration date. Tomorrow, next week, next month, or next year is not guaranteed to be ours. Those of us blessed with time enough will live to see every drop of our youthfulness fade away. It matters not when our expiration date arrives, the world will not stop turning. It will carry on without us. So today, this precious moment while you still have breath, why diminish the quality of your life because of the severe unexpected that fooled you into feelings of hopelessness? The dreadfulness that is sadness does not have to move in and take over your life forever. It does not have to own your life. You are far greater. It should not be allowed to cut another path of destruction through your life. Your mind should always be a peaceful place. Prolonged sadness robs us of our ability to see oncoming destruction more often than not. No innocent person who was forced to endure severe physical and emotional hardship should be living a life controlled by feelings of helplessness. In spite of the severity of your pain, you still have there in your humanity the greatness of the positive power that was given to you at the moment of your conception. Those well preserved cruel memories that can sometimes bring so much resentment you feel as if you could tear this entire world apart is not the full to capacity power that you need in your life. Those emotions are way too toxic to your heart, your mind, your entire being. If you keep giving into these negative emotions, the first life that you will tear apart is your own. But if you are willing to take all of that negative energy and exchange it for the positive power in you instead, the first life that will be blessed is your own. That is a guarantee from God, the Almighty.

Great are the tender mercies of God. Taking your own life for granted will leave you with feeling of emptiness. Your life was not intended to be divided up by inner conflicts. You were created for greatness. Become relentless in your pursuit of happiness. Why deny yourself the positive greatness that is so much a part of your humanity? Your life should always be progressive, not regressive. I have never seen or heard of anyone who was able to use sadness to renew their spirit. What I have seen is sadness at a suicidal rate. Some people are the way that they are, are where they are in life, doing what they are because they don't know who they are. There are as many different causes as there are people, but for a lot of depressed, confused people, they are the way that they are because another human being lacking compassion at their most selfish decided to prey on their innocent soul, turning their young mind into a junkyard. As a result, these precious innocent human beings grew up as I did, seeing themselves as having less value. The loss of your best life is an unaffordable loss.

We know that time is a great equalizer, but don't wait to see what kind of adjustments life is going to make to those who did you wrong before you can move on with your life. The Almighty has everything under his control. A fuller acceptance and greater love of self will most certainly further your healing beautifully. Even an hour of sadness takes us too far away from our true self. Feelings of sadness are a part of being human, but they should not become a permanent part of your humanity. That's when other problems are drawn into us to set. Only positive pleasurable changes should be allowed to set into us. Too often, without realizing that we are, we end up helping others to exploit us. It's like drinking a double dose of poison. Ban negative behavior from all areas of your life. You don't need to, neither do you have to live with viciousness. Until you respect yourself in all the ways you should be, you cannot expect anyone else here on earth to show you the respect that you deserve as a human being. People take their cue from you. We tell people by our actions or by our inactions how to treat us. You will never be taken seriously until you love yourself seriously. God is waiting for you to do your part. With trust and faith in God, you can plan more carefully your best future starting today. Your confidence in your God-given abilities will grow like a running plant fresh from the earth. You can become so much bigger than your regrets. Be renewed. Be kind to yourself. A life in limbo is certainly not the best life that you can offer yourself. You should delight in your own life in spite of life's cruel circumstances. Choose wisely. Recommend yourself for the best. Recommend yourself for joy and use it to mark the end of your sorrow. Do it while you are still vibrant. The cruel circumstance that you can never change should not be allowed to stop you before you are forced by time to withdraw from life. I had to find out in the most difficult of ways how painful the rejection of true self can become. On more than one occasion in my adult life, I felt in my heart and soul that the decisions that I was making in my private life might be the wrong choice. I chose instead to reject my God-given instinct and dove head first into some of the most disappointing days of my life, a rejection of self I could not afford. Regardless of how you were taught or who it was that taught you to think of yourself as insignificant, this is a mentality that will never work to your benefit. Thinking of yourself as being insignificant will always send the wrong message to everyone in your environment. Having a bad mentality is sure to work against you in ways that will put you more out of harmony with the things in life that should be enjoyable to you. It is a fact that our thoughts dictate our actions. Therefore, not thinking highly of yourself is not a way to draw to your life those things that will bring you the most comfort, the better understanding, the most kindness and the most joy. If, like me, you were abused as a child, perhaps you are still not aware that besides murder, obviously, one of the great evils that happen as the result of child abuse is how most children's God-given independent thinking that was meant to keep their lives uplifted is replaced with the same self-hatred of their abuser. A person who loves their own humanity would never prey on a fellow human being. You did not enter the world hating yourself. Somewhere along the roads of life, the cruelties applied to your life taught you to think of yourself in ungodly ways. Having even an ounce of contempt for your own humanity is not the true nature of your soul, I assure you. It is sinful to hate God's creation. Having the gift of life does not grant you permission to hate yourself. Self hatred is the ultimate disrespect. The lead of anyone who refuses to respect your life is certainly not a lead that you should be following. The intelligence given to you by God is far greater than the evil ideas of any devil. Think about this for a minute. What if you had to drive to a place you had never been before to find a specific address? While you are driving around searching for this address, you came upon two roads laid directly before you. One road is named "Misery Road" and the other is named "Happiness Road." Which one of these two roads would you be more curious about? Which one would you choose to help you find your way to where you want to get to? Most people I know, in spite of their dissatisfaction with themselves would be far more interested in driving down the Happiness Road. Living a life of misery will never get you to the places in life that will bring you to true happiness. Sacrificing your entire life to the kinds of suffering you have the power to change is not the kind of big difference you should be making in your life. You have the rich inner power to help rescue your own life from a storm of darkness. Yes you can! You really can. You are able to move your life back into the light where it belongs. You are an earthly treasure that should be living a life of God-given pleasures. Your life matters. Don't throw it away. Most victims of abuse show very little of the types of interest that they should in their own lives and are not even aware of this. Their inaction is killing them. Some people have accepted the relentless emotional pain and deep anger that is a result of some of life's most bitter disappointments as a permanent part of who they are. You should feel safe and satisfied with your life as you live under the provision of faith and the power of your own human positiveness. I am another living proof that it is possible to emerge from sadness victoriously. If you had seen the emotional mess I once was, you would understand why I know for a fact that *with God, all things are possible.* I taught myself how to be grateful for every drop of breath in my body, how to admire His great wonder-working powers all the way to the better person that I am today. This miracle is possible for you too. This miracle is yours in waiting. You are under no obligation to sadness. You don't have to be sad to be human. Sadness requires too much over time that you will never be paid positively for. Commitment and a sense of personal responsibility to sadness is one of the cruelest ways to diminish the quality of your life. Your mind, your soul, your spirit, the emotions of your heart should all be in a rhythm of peaceful oneness. The earth was created to showcase your life in a divine spiritual light that is more beautiful and more powerful than that of the sun in the skies above you. You are a magnificent creation. If you will allow yourself to imagine greatness you can look in any mirror and see the reality of it. You were created to celebrate life as much as life is to celebrate you. That is another reason why grief should never find you easily. It will take full unfair advantage of you as it holds back your life. Sadness is not an emotion that leaves enough breathing space to allow you to keep thinking highly of yourself. Sadness will kill your days four-by-four unless you decide to fight against it. People care less about themselves when they are experiencing sadness. Yet despite how deep into its grip you are, at this moment you still possess the strength to pull yourself away from the mess of it all. You can move from sadness to gladness. You must! Sadness will never be kind to you. You have to be kind to yourself. This will be the most valuable move of your life. You are able to make the most important differences in your life. You can remove your life from this stagnant toxic bondage. You can have the life that is perfect for you, and you can have it starting right now. Why wait? Why not accept the richness of the miracle working powers in you that is still connected to God Almighty? God is my witness that faith is a far more powerful way to live. Let positive thoughts become you. Don't spend the rest of your life wasting the powers of your mind on the negative thinking. You are too valuable to live that way. Turning what remains of your life over to sadness is the same as turning yourself over to an enemy then demanding they do with you whatever it takes to destroy you and bring them the sickest satisfaction. From the time that I was old enough to see God in every living thing, I realized that dangerous animals were not meant to include humans among them. Abuse by human hands should never include your own. You were not created a dangerous animal. I promise you that if you use the fullness of faith to celebrate your life everyday, God will take notice of your gratitude. Having the right attitude will make an enormous difference in your life that you will love. Understanding the significance of your own life will keep you from being washed away by the tides of sorrow. Understanding the value of you will work miracles to reset your life. You can still have the best new beginning any human being has ever had. Please want the best for you—I beg of you. Want it bad enough to see straight. One of the quickest ways to amputate your spirit is to allow sadness to defeat you. Accepting defeat is not what your mind, hand, heart and spirit was created to do. The very fact that you exist gives you a direct connection to your Creator, the original positive power happiness Maker. Your desire for happiness should never end. I don't want it to take you as long as it took me to get up from the place I was knocked down. I know what it feels like to be a tortured soul. For many years the very expressions on my face showed the signs of a tortured soul. There was a time in my life when the bravest of souls would walk up to me and tell me to smile. For example, years ago, I was shopping at the Lexington Market in Baltimore, Maryland when a gentleman walked up to me and asked, "Why did you put on make-up this morning?" I was not only puzzled by this unusual question, I was very surprised. Not only was his question quite intrusive, it reeked of stupidity—I thought. But instead of allowing myself to get upset right away, I thought it fair to ask him, "Why?" He was quick to inform me that he thought women wore make up to make themselves not only look better but feel better about themselves as well. As soon as he said that to me, I wanted to cut him off, but fortunately for him, before I could, he decided to push his luck and express himself further, telling me that if I am going to enter the public looking so sad, would be better if I did not wear any make up. He pointed out that it is wrong to waste cosmetics on a face as sad as mine. Clearly, this man saw it as something too good for a sad face. I was too shocked at his boldness (or courage, if you will) to do anything about it. I had a few choice words on the tip of my tongue, but his comments left me speechless. I knew he meant well, but I also felt his approach was the wrong one. He was acting on his own ignorance. I felt then and still feel that his concern should have been for the human soul behind the pretty cosmetics instead of the other way around. Years later, after my soul began to heal from the childhood assaults, I looked back on that day and realized there must have been something about the expression on my face, my body language or just the way that I carried myself, in general, that told him he could approach me with such boldness and get away with it. His words were anything but nourishing to my soul at the time, nevertheless, the effect of his careless, thoughtless words had on my life worked to my advantage. Still to this day, every time I glide my favorite lip gloss gently across my lips or apply my special lash extending mascara, I remind myself sadness should never again be a part of the make-up that I wear. In spite of the blood anger that I felt towards him at the time for his thoughtless comments, I will be forever grateful to that stranger who I am sure will leave this world not knowing the positive contribution he made to my life. Intentional or unintentional, his careless words forced me to think about the direction of my life more carefully. For me it was a moment of clarity he was not aware he volunteered for. I have also learned since then that if you are someone who is beaten down on the inside, try as you might to hide this reality from the rest of the world, there are still people who can see it on the outside of you and use your emotional misfortune to take liberties with your life. They will most certainly use it against you if you give them the opportunity to do so. You could spend your entire life here on this earth being a victim of cruelty unless you decide you are not going to take being abused anymore. I must tell you that back then when I encountered the Lexington Market wise guy, I was an emotional maxed-out young woman. The stress of unresolved issues was slowly eroding my true character. The nightmare flashbacks were an almost fatal addiction. I did not realize how much I was stepping on my own life. I have always been proud of the fact that I am not one of those unfortunate souls that have been wasted by substance abuse. On the other hand, I too was being destroyed by the toxic emotions that came as a result of the cruel remembrances. I wanted so desperately to break away from it. It was killing me, especially when I recalled certain memories, but I just did not know how to. What I did know was this. There is no positive benefit in toxic emotions. It is very important to have inner peace. Without it, we are only half truth. I was being just as destructive to my mind, my spirit and my body as an alcoholic or someone who is addicted to other types of drugs. It is important to add that I really did not know how completely sadness can destroy someone's life. I wanted and needed so much to get back the self-respect that was robbed from me at such a tender age. Whether you are someone who believes that there is a power in the universe greater than yourself or not, the one thing I pray I am able to do as you read this is to raise your awareness of self so high you will be able to see the value and the preciousness of your own humanity and refuse to be dominated by pain. The fact remains, a hundred years from now, human beings will continue to make mistakes, and those mistakes will continue to be a lot bigger when unresolved issues are in charge of choice. No abuser can undo their dirty deeds. That is one of the reasons why how clean you feel should not be left up to your abuser. Begin your mission to put your mind back into the healthy place it belongs. You were born with all of the right powerful ingredients to bring together and start running your own life better. You are just one of the ways God shows His love. He is waiting to take from you the pain you have been holding on to. You don't have to endure endlessly. Get serious about your total spiritual healing. All you have to want is what's best for yourself to prevent the inner turmoil. Some people hold onto anger and hate as their way of surviving, not realizing how costly this bad choice can be. Anyone will benefit from a healthier outlook on life. Dragging around any garbage that was forced into your life will drag you down and force you out of the normalcy of your life. The grim will not just drag you to the rim. It will chew you up. Get gutsy. You are strong enough to do life sweeter. Accept your divine protection and come back from the adrift. You can overcome and increase your strength now. Leave the disturbing behind and open up your heart and mind to God's best opportunities. You can do so much more for yourself. Defend and protect your life from unclean spirits. The habits that serve no good purpose should be made history. It is possible to live a wonderful life. Some people are so emotionally shattered they live every moment wondering where or how they will end up. This does not have to be the case with you. Know that you are still in God's favor. Trust that you are still in God's favor. The powerful effort that went into your creation is still available for your use in every level of your life. You are not alone. Don't get lost in doubt. Supporting the habit of sadness is a deadly addiction. It's an alarmingly dangerous thing to do. The ways of sadness is very polluting. It will always be a pollution not a solution, deep sadness slowly pulls some people away until the best of their lives are lying in ruin. I truly believe that regardless of how painful the emotional trauma was that you suffered that brought you to the place of deep sadness, you can still overcome it to live the better of your life. You just have to decide that you are going to stop allowing unresolved issues to choose for you. It is very difficult to make the choices that are best for your life when your focus is elsewhere. Whatever the harm is that was done to your life and whatever types of mistakes you yourself might have made with your life as a result, those mistakes could get a lot bigger if you keep giving them room to grow. That is what sadness does. It provides growing room for the negative. There are too many victims of cruel circumstance that are still living in a mode of unforgiveness. Any unwillingness to forgive others will make it less likely that you will ever forgive yourself for any of your human mistakes. If you yourself were an evil person who wanted to poison someone, you would not drink the poison yourself, would you? Of course not! You are not stupid. So why then are you poisoning yourself with the toxic emotions of anger? Your toxic emotions won't kill your offender. It will kill you. Unforgiveness and all of the emotional anguish that comes with holding on to memories that are cutting into your soul will keep robbing you of the positive nature you were sent into the world with. Why not spend the rest of your life being thankful you were able to survive the cruelty? The refreshments, the newness that you need is there within your power. You must have faith that your positiveness can be fully restored. You can faith your life so much better than you realize. You can use the power of faith to restore your life to its earthly best. You can restore laughter, joy, peace and love. You can have it all just as your Creator intended. And in case you still don't believe in your own strength just take an even closer look at the fact you were able to survive to see this day in spite of it all. But it's not enough to survive if you still don't understand the enormous value of your own precious life. You were not created cheaply. You have nothing in common with the trash that was dumped on you. Harvest the positive power in you and use it. As long as you are still alive there is no misfortune that can stand up to your God-given inner strength, especially at harvest time. Who is going to keep you from the love of God if you are determined to accept it? No one! No one in this world can stop you from living a life that is full of positive powerfulness. God's love is not a first-come-first-served kind of love. God's love will always be available to you. Three hundred and sixty five days a year, day or night, for all eternity, you need to accept that it is how it is. The greatest most powerful unconditional love in the entire universe is yours for accepting. Please don't give up on your life. You are a powerful living miracle. Just think—you are only one of six billion people in the world today. Yet there is no one else on this earth that is exactly like you. We are all one of a kind. No human life can be replaced with another. No set of identical twins are actually truly identical in every way. You are as original as God Himself. You are a one of a kind human being that can be found no where else on earth. You are an original best. No other human being on earth can replace you. You are that special, that unique, that precious. You are a fantastic creation. You are such an original miraculous magnificent creation of God's. It is a fact that no one can erase your originality. Even after death you will still be an original. You were molded by divine faith, uniquely designed by love. The opportunity of life itself was meant to be used as a source of joy, not a source of mass destruction. As a former pain collector who experienced great increase, I can tell you that collecting every ounce of emotional pain that every evil doer with their unhealthy distorted view of life introduce you to will never build a strong foundation for your life. Unfortunately, we are not always aware of the deductions depression is making in our lives until the day we begin to look for the missing years but unable to get them back. By the time most people are forty years young, they realize that time waits for no one. You cannot escape sadness until you come to the realization that you are far too valuable to allow it into your soul permanently. A peaceful soul is a joyful soul. Having a peaceful soul will supply you with the special nourishment your mind needs. Sadness, depression, neither of these deserves to have a life at the expense of yours. They should never be built into your future. Don't give these dangerous emotions a life. You can go beyond the selfishness that is sadness. Sadness is controlling. It's very inhibiting. It makes unaffordable deductions. It demands lasting negative impacts. It brain washes you into betraying your own trust, your own faith. It can damage the human heart in more ways than you can imagine and often do. It takes away confidence and keeps you from making the best most lasting contributions to your own life, contributions that you should be making everyday. It is an ugly web of deceit. That is why emotional pain should never be a priority in your life. End it! End it now! Replace that priority with the inner strength cruel circumstances told you you did not have. Trust that you can reap from an evolving transformation. You were not pulled at random from thin air. You are here because you were thought out, created and emerged from the mighty hands of God, the Greatest Power that exists anywhere. Should you be blessed to live for another one hundred years, you will still have that same divine power within that you were created with and the same God-given permission to harvest it. As long as we are living in this human body we will make mistakes. There is no question about it, some mistakes more honest than others. Even so, there is full forgiveness from the ultimate Intelligence. Give faith in God a try. He is more than willing to forgive us for the years wasted in bitterness, rage and sadness. It is possible to meet the challenges of life faith on and accept yourself as the awesome miracle that you are. Once you open up your mind to your rightful positive way of thinking, it will become as natural to you as the breath of life that you are still being gifted. Your positive new ways of thinking will show. Everyone in your environment will notice. You are sure to draw into your life what contribute. Contribute positiveness and draw to your life more of the same. You can evolve from any types of emotional anguish. Happiness should never be out of your character. Appreciate your own life more. If you will start doing that right now, I promise you that a lovelier brand new you will emerge. You will be the most pleasant, most wonderful surprise of your life. Over the years, I have taught myself through extremely painful emotional difficulties that the effects of any rising painful memories should never rise higher than my faith in God. We all go through changes in our lives that can sometimes make it difficult to retain full faith, which is why when I see people who are still searching for a way out of their sadness, I find myself praying for them to discover the full positive power in their humanity. So many of our fellow human beings are not aware how much they are loved simply because they are not open to the idea of a Divine unconditional Love. Instead, their main focus is on the self-punishment that will continue to weaken them further. At the same time, there are, unfortunately, people who will choose misery over positive change because they are so very terrified of going past the old to the new, preferring instead to live with the difficulties that they have become accustomed to, out right refusing to allow themselves the inner peace that every decent human being deserves to have. I realize that because we are alive, complexities will arise, but you can use the beautiful sides of life to keep those complicated issues from having less of a devastating impact. You have a remarkable mind that you can use to help give yourself all the best. You can thrive. You can be as successful as you want to be. You can start living your life in the positive power that is yours to have forever instead of in the mind muck that sadness can sometimes bring. You can reshape your mind back into a better you just by including into your life more of the things that make you smile. Having faith in your own wonderful abilities can be such a powerful thing. Faith can afford all of your good wishes. There is no limit to the joy you will receive. You can laugh everyday. I am not necessarily suggesting you climb on the roof of your house at night for a musical summer picnic to create a historical moment, although that would be a wonderful way to celebrate summer if you have a flat roof and could do it safely. What I am suggesting, however, is that you give yourself the new start that you deserve. Sadness can be so mentally and physically tiring. God gave you a remarkable mind. Make it a safe environment again so that you can put it to better use. You don't have to live the rest of your life enduring the heavy weight of sadness. You don't need such a heavy burden to remind yourself that you are made of flesh and blood. There are a billion beautiful ways to do that. I don't like to see good useful things being wasted, especially now that I am so much wiser than I used to be. As human beings errors will be made, even so there are areas in our lives that we can change that will make the world a much better place for all of us to live. For example, a simple compliment given in the right spirit to a stranger can circle the entire globe in one day. You alone can set off a chain reaction of sweet positiveness. You can sooth the soul and mind of millions of people all over the world just by being a pleasant human being. Obviously the opposite is true as well. We can all make this planet earth of God's a much better place to live. Simple small changes can bring stunningly good results. Besides our Creator who is always a sure thing, you are the best thing that you have. No matter where your spiritual faith lies, without inner peace, your life's journey will never include your very best. Any aggressiveness towards your own life should never include your betrayal. Living a sad, lonely, depressed life when you are able to do better for yourself is a betrayal of self. Your positive human power was not given to you in a limited way. Positive power is limitless. You were created with a lot more power than you have yet to harvest. Some of our fellow human beings are so busy trivializing their own lives and giving into negative thoughts that they neglect to secure their happiness. Leaving yourself vulnerable to destruction is most unwise. You need more than a little happiness on the surface to fully enjoy your fast moving days. You need that deep in the mind, heart and soul kind of happiness to make it really count. You owe it to yourself to experience that as-real-as-it-gets joy that is born from true inner peace. No human being worthy of happiness should have to die in order to have peace. It is very important to have true inner peace while you are still in the land of the living. Having inner peace allows us to make better choices for ourselves. Being harsh with yourself will not help to strengthen you in any way. Calm gentle ways will preserve you better. Whether you appreciate it or not, every single thing about the way that you were created is special and uniquely beautiful. You are a treasure, God's permanent investment. You are wonderfully made. You were created from what will never die. Love never dies. From this powerful source you came to life. Your days here on earth are meant to be enhanced by goodness. You are not living by your own power alone.

Most of us alive today will continue to have those days when things don't seem very promising to us and the last thing we feel like doing is standing up. Even so, giving up is not a path to follow, no matter how sad and disappointed you feel. The thing to remember is that you are not hopeless. Life's disappointments don't make you less valuable. They can't. Living hopeful is one of the best ways to put your extra intelligence to work for you. Allowing your mind to become weak and disorganized due to prolonged sadness is always going to be diminishing. Why spend the rest of your life feeling as if a part of your soul is missing when you should be experiencing shivers of joy. Check out the world around you. Take an honest closer look. There are millions of fellow human beings who are missing an arm, a leg, perhaps both arms or both legs. This unfortunate reality does not make them less human. They are not less valuable. Some of these courageous human beings become even more powerful than they were before because they refuse to give up. If you notice, most people who are born physically challenged are far more powerful in their determination to live life to its fullest than the able bodies among us. Most of these brilliant fellow human beings refuse to waste too much precious time being envious and feeling sorry for themselves. They know how to choose good. They know why it is important to choose good. I love the determination of those people who refuse to hide themselves away because the rest of the world tells them that they are not perfect enough to look at. They force the rest of us to accept the reality of their existence.

There is not one perfect human being among us. We can pretend all we want to. Pretending won't make it so. We are all flawed. I bet you can guess what I am going to say next. Some of us more flawed than others. Some people are terrifyingly flawed on the inside where it is not obvious at first sight. So we are not put off, especially if they are very pretty or very handsome. The so-called "physical" perfection, we not only accept these seemingly perfect people right away, we give very willingly and generously our best smiles. I must tell you that I am not suggesting that giving a smile to someone who is nice looking and easy on the eyes is the wrong thing to do. Jesus told us to love one another. This was because Jesus wished for us to carry on His peaceful ways. But let's be honest. If someone is very beautiful or very handsome, there are more than a few people willing to trip over themselves in the race to make themselves available for their convenience, and all because of the outward appearance. They could care less about the contents of their soul. On the other hand, when some of us encounter someone whose flaws we are able to see immediately, we either look away, look at them with fear and disgust, or we are ready to throw them a pity party, when most of the time they don't really need our pity at all. What they do need all of the time is our respect, our understanding and our acceptance of them as human beings that despite any physical challenges deserve our respect. We can do so much to make this world that we live in a better place. We waste so much time being preoccupied with the wrong things. How about you? Are you someone who is willing to rise to a wiser way of doing life and make it effective immediately? The human mind is mega powerful. We are such a fantastic creation. We can and have done so many great things. We have made as many positive contributions to this planet as there are children, and yet because of unhappiness in the lives of too many people, some eventually descend into the embracing madness of daily negative thoughts instead of getting tired of who they have become. As we know, the madness of negative thoughts is a tragedy that began with the first human. Those negative thinkers who are not as far gone, are still at a great distance from their true spiritual identity. It is a fact that our brain is at its performing best when we are thinking positively. The joy that one experiences from doing so makes a very uplifting, rich difference. I promise you that this is true. Having positive thoughts everyday will not only delight and be even more beneficial to everyone around you, it will truly enrich every area of your life. You may not think of yourself as a worthwhile cause. Even so, God knows that you are. He created you. He knows how truly valuable you are. Were it possible for you to sit down with your Creator face-to-face and listen to Him explain to you the wonderful ways in which you were thought out and the loving effort that was placed into the original you, I believe these truths would return you to your life as it were intended to be. It is because you are a creation of the ultimate love why your life should be nothing less than breathtakingly beautiful. You are a major life decision of God's. Live your life wisely. Why not positive power out the inaccuracies and be known for your peacefulness and extraordinary joyful personality. Good people from all walks of life will seek your company. They will come to your pleasantness to be embraced by your warmth. They will come from every corner of the earth. They will flock to you as bees do to honey. Live wonderfully wiser so that only the good will seek your company. Start experiencing life as it should be. It is because you are a once-in-a-lifetime opportunity why you cannot afford to throw you away. Broken? Tell hell, "NO!" and unlock your God-given positive power before it's your time to fly back to eternity. Don't lie down and die like some helpless injured animal in the forest. You have a place in the heart of God. Stay in sight of your dreams that by faith is sure to be made a reality. Don't waste your once-in-a-lifetime opportunity. We have all seen people who must be aided by a walking cane. It's a must if they want to take some of the pressure off. Faith works in very much the same way. What do I mean by that? Well, people who have used a walking cane have faith that it will do for them exactly what they expect it to do, and it does. True faith has stronger legs than us. It will walk you through the difficult times. Faith in God can do so much more than we are able to do for ourselves. It is your best vehicle to realization. God is not twenty percent accurate and twenty percent perfect. God is one hundred percent accurate and one hundred percent perfect. This perfect supernatural full of miracles power has the right medicine. God never loses faith in Himself or in us. We are the ones who lose faith in Him and in ourselves. Too much is at stake when we don't know what we want out of life or in what direction to go. Without God, we are nothing. Without this mighty power, we don't have a prayer. Without the mercy of God, we are lost. We are blessed to have within our reach a loving power that is so full of mercy and forgiveness. There is no one on earth or in heaven that can wipe away God's mercy from your life. With God you are always welcome to miracles. No one can remove your trust in the Almighty. Never give up. Never stop believing you are right in the path of miracles. You are a precious resource. You cannot afford to throw yourself away on negative thinking. Be very careful how you think. Our very thoughts have a way of coming to life on us. Beautiful is what happens when we allow the Almighty to direct our path. This suit of flesh and life within was given to us as a source of joy. Everyday that we are alive should be a delicious celebration of life. It is the bad choices that we sometimes make in our adult lives that oppress us and lead to mental and emotional restlessness. Nothing should keep you from seeing how God created you. Every moment of your life is precious. We did not come to life foolishly, yet as human beings, that is what we do best. The few holidays that we set aside every year that gives some of us, if only for a day, the opportunity to forget our troubles, are simply not enough joy time. It's not enough time away from the pressures of life. To rest the mind, body and soul, we need a lot more joy time. We need more rest, more gentleness, but most importantly, we need more love in every area of our lives. Any kind of war begins in the human mind first before it is put into action on the outside where every one else can see it. There are people whose inner wars the rest of us never get to see until the fatal results that come without the opportunity to reserve it. Many people all over the world die from worrying everyday. Some died because they were so good at not seeking the help that they so desperately needed. We need to eliminate all of the excuses we give to ourselves for starting our own inner wars so that we can receive our miracle rewards. It is our God-given right as human beings to live joyfully. Jehovah is loving and faithful. This is proven to us everyday. The earth is still being given the power to sustain us. We should always be wonderfully wise and open our minds and heart to the glory of the Almighty. Even the bad decisions that we sometimes make without meaning to don't only effect us. It almost always affects those around us in one form or another. Challenge your self to a more successful life. What greater privilege is there than the privilege of life? This world that we are sharing would be as Jehovah God intended it to be if we would all strengthen our minds and hearts with the needed provision of peace and happiness. No one was born into the world to become carriers of grief. We need to put the great value on our lives that it is, when we are willing to do so, blessings will come to us. The very beats of your heart should be more than enough to remind you what's important. Reality should not be processed through emotional pain contacts for the rest of your life. Sadness should not come to rest on you permanently. Anyone determined to continue making room in their lives for sadness might as well stamp "DELAYED" on their forehead for the rest of the world to see. This is what prolonged sadness does. It delays, and in the most severe cases, destroys life all together. Its decaying effects are merciless, but this is a preventable robbery. Anyone can emerge from sadness victorious. You don't have to go through life a prisoner of nervousness. You are a glorious, magnificent being. You won't go to some other hell hotter than sadness if you refuse to continue embracing sadness. Living with depression is blistering enough. Those painful blisters on your heart and in your mind are some of the reasons you should not be afraid to step out of the darkness. Depression is such a bad connection. You can remove yourself from it. You have a powerful, kind, loving connection that is yours to use every moment of everyday for the rest of your life. Why should you continue living a life of sadness when you have within you the positive power to make a peace plan for yourself? There is wondrous healing in your willingness to seek the better path that will move you forward. Some people are afraid of the darkness while others are afraid to come out of the darkness. I believe that deep inside of every sad heart is a yearning for happiness. This is especially true for people who refuse to discuss their true feelings. Jesus encouraged kindness. Mercifully, there are still fellow human beings throughout the world who live by His encouraging words and are more than willing to put His teachings into action by lending a helping hand to anyone in need. As grateful as most people are, myself included, that such compassion still exists in today's ever-increasing, violent world, I must mention how unfortunate I think it is that so many people who were abused in childhood grow up to be more respectful of others than they are of themselves. There is the constant need to make everyone else happy while their own needs are forgotten. Lost in the insecurity that is unless they please others they themselves will not be worthy to receive love, they feel they must be willing to make sacrifices in every area of their lives otherwise who is going to love a vulnerable soul such as themselves? God does. He not only knows you by name, He loves you with the purest of unconditional love. Jesus Christ has already made the ultimate sacrifice for every area of your life. You need not continue living with those sad feelings of insecurities that are sure to continue dragging you down. Always remember that you were created by the same powerful, loving hands that created every other human being both past and present. You are as good as every other living breathing fellow human being. I am not telling you not to be kind to others. What I am saying to you is this, you don't have to live your life as a sacrificial lamb, no matter how badly you were hurt in your innocent, helpless years, especially because you were hurt in your most innocent, helpless years. True love can not be bought. True friendship cannot be bought. I will be forever grateful to every single human being who contributes positively to my life, but gone are the days when I lived my life to please everyone but me. Gone are those days of blighting mentality when I punished myself because of the sins others committed against me. Get your mind right. Take stock of your life. Vision for yourself a sweeter future made possible by your faith in the power that is greater than us and the wiser decisions that it will direct you to make. The many positive results will amaze you.

A brand new you, a brand new life is only your willingness away. You are a body of powerful knowledge waiting to be harvested. You will learn so much more about your own humanity the moment that you start refusing to take your own life for granted. The poor choices that can sometimes happen as the result of deep sadness will become a thing of the past. I know first hand that it takes faith and courage to continue living after experiencing the kinds of emotional pain you did not know existed in such intensity. The good news is emotional pain does not have to take away your desire to live or your right to choose the salvation of happiness for the rest of your breaths. You can take your life back from the disturbing. Truly, you can. You really don't need permission from any other person to be happy. Your life's best chance of a resurrection here on earth while you are still wearing your suit of flesh lies within your determination to exercise faith. In order to receive your blessings you must take yourself out of the muck mentality. God will always have your best interest at heart.

Remove the wall from your mind. You were born free. Now live free, free from mental anguish, free from abuse of any kind. You are here on this earth because it is God's will that you be here. You are the will of God in action. Your life was not given without a positive purpose. No human being has ever been created without a positive purpose. There are many reasons why so many people in the world today are living with frustration, anxiety, and anger. I believe one of those reasons people are so mentally messed up and out of sorts is because they don't know what their true purpose in life is. If they knew what it was I believe it would change their lives for the better. The answer to many of our questions lies within a faithful prayer. Can you imagine living the rest of your life wandering aimlessly, not knowing what you should really be doing with your life, while in the meantime, giving permission to the negative energies that invade, rearrange, and control lives? You should never imagine a single day of your life without purpose. This is not to suggest you become a workaholic. As I mentioned before, we don't take enough time to stop and appreciate the miracle of life. Most of us are just way too busy wasting precious energy on the things that should not be a part of our existence in the first place. Yesterday is now gone forever, but if it were a joyful day for you, then yes, why not hold the sweet memories of yesterday in your heart forever. But if yesterday were a painful day for you and you no longer have any use for those memories, why not try to leave those painful memories in yesterday where they belong? God does heal broken hearts.

I consider the gift of life to be a miracle that hangs on the mercy of God. Worrying about the things we do not have within our power to change is a dreadful waste of time. Worrying can also cause great injury to the body as well as the soul. A broken spirit, regardless of why it was broken, can cause us to make mistakes, the kind of mistakes that we might find very difficult to live with, that in turn can cause even more grief. As long as we are living in the flesh, we will make mistakes from time to time. I am not talking about those fellow human beings among us who go out and deliberately hurt someone else for no reason other than to be evil. Those kinds of people who enjoy doing evil things to others are determined to remain in Satan's army. I am talking about good, God-fearing people who sometimes make mistakes. They didn't mean to. I have found that anyone living with an agitated heart lacks the ability to make sound judgment. I am certain that God had good reasons for telling us, "Fret not thyself." It is all too true that depression interrupts our connection to God. Most of us are wise enough to keep company with only those good people who we know can and will make positive contributions to our lives in one form or another. Why then would you want to keep company with depression for the rest of your life? Toxic emotions have a wide range of illnesses. Why live sickly if you don't have to? Keeping your heart happy is the best medicine you can offer yourself. This entire planet earth is your living room. There is a lot of room here for you to enjoy. There is so much to see, so much to experience, so much to love. God approves of this place for us for our pleasure. Be wise. Don't miss out. Enjoy the time that you are being given to stay here. Only God knows what this planet will be like a hundred years from now. Happiness is a wonderful experience no one should miss out on. Don't make anxiety a permanent part of your life. The happiness that comes from inner peace is my favorite prosperity. It is the only human emotion that is guaranteed to not only add years to your own life but to the lives of those in your environment. The fact that this very necessary prosperity brings lives together should tell us that happy is the normal right way of life as it was meant to be. Inner peace works wonders to preserve the human body. Giving sadness the freedom to direct our life's path has never lead to any true, lasting, positive gain. Like you, I am a flesh-dwelling being who made the conscious decision to restore my mental health to its full power. I needed to give myself the understanding and compassion I did not receive during my formative years and beyond. I did not want to suffer by my own hands, or should I say, by my own mind anymore. I feel blessed to have come out of my suffering with a much healthier understanding of life, a wonderfully different way of understanding life that will always help me to make the most of my place in time. The fact that I am no longer living under the dark influences of sadness leaves my life open for full blessings. I now consider my soul a gathering place for positive influences. As you now know, that was not always the case. Fortunately for me, gone are the days when my preoccupation with my blemished covered legs kept me in front of full length mirrors for hours feeling sorry for myself. I was unable to stop the seriously painful haunting memories of yesteryears that bore their way into my precious life's time. I still had courage, but was lacking the right know-how I needed to find the best way to use it. Amid the clutter of horror reruns that kept punishing me, I found it too difficult to spare the time needed to fully appreciate my own life. My mind was crowded with invaders of the worst kind. My mind needed the kind of crowd control that only God could give me. I was so caught up in past troubles that I was not able to control these relentless thieves as they stole from my life. I was too busy living my life in depression to see the erosion. It was the kind of linking up I needed to live without. As much as I love God for removing my life from the total human ignorance that surrounded me. I was still not sure of the best way to let myself out of the despicable memories. My body finally had the God-given freedom that I came into the world entitled to, but my mind was not free from the hell I had endured. I was unable to come to terms with the cruel thoughtless acts of human madness and violence that forced me to live in permanently blemished skin. It was a time in my life when all was not well with my soul, even though I was no longer a tormented child living in an environment of human predators. I was still the recipient of oppression. In my mind, I could still see and hear the adults blaming the child that I was for the horrible abuse I suffered. I was finally mercifully free from the human ignorance and cruelties that I had so much contempt for, yet there I was, still a prisoner of my abusers' sins. I still had no real authority over my own life, and unlike the days I was forced to run for my life, there was nowhere to run from the bitter memories, and no one who understood what I was forced as a child to live through. I was intertwined with the set rules of turmoil and was being hauled along. Those cruelties recorded in the history of my life were not my fault, of course, and I knew in my heart even as a child that I did nothing to deserve the enormous amount of abuse that I suffered. No child wants to be abused. No child invites crimes against their humanity, knowing this was not enough at the time to keep from being invaded. Those cruel memories slammed me so hard and so often, looking back from whence I came to these overcoming days, it is more than a little obvious. Only the prayers I was able to pray kept me standing, but I needed to reshape my thinking. My entire life needed a resurrection. My life desperately needed to fall gently back into the place my Creator had intended for it to be. The long torturous journey needed to end. It was time for a peaceful inner spirit. My entire being was starving for the vital nourishment that inner peace provides. I was concentrating on past evils instead of appreciating my own breaths of life. God was doing His best to get my attention. Thankfully, He was doing it in the gentlest of ways. But I was just too busy suffering inner deaths to take notice. It was because Jehovah did not have my full attention why I was so confused about how to turn things around in my favor. In my case, I needed to just give it all to Jehovah God and let Him set things right. After all, those who become an enemy of God's children, He becomes an enemy of them. I desperately needed to take the pressure off and lovingly reward myself with the urgent restoration I needed.

Whatever the tragedy was that you encountered, the blight of sadness does not have to follow you for the remaining days of your life. Moving on from the intensity of emotional pain takes the kind of strength and bravery that was included into your humanity. We came into the world empty handed, but there is nothing empty about the power of the human mind. The abundance of positive power that you have yet to harvest is a power that you can use towards the building of a brand new positive way of life. There is much more of life to explore and enjoy. You are accountable for your own happiness. God can provide us a feast. Whether we decide to eat from the generous feast our Heavenly Father provides for us or we decide to starve ourselves to death is up to us. We should all live with the constant reminder that each day that passes is a day lost to us forever. The traumatic events you were blessed to be able to survive should not be given a chance to come back and join in your future. It will take over. It's a sacrifice you should not make. I have seen depression take control of many lives in many different ways. Mental anguish began body-slamming them before they could gather themselves up. Everyday that you are still alive gives you the opportunity to find the right escape route out of emotional difficulties. You can move out of the feelings of madness to feelings of gladness. Happiness makes us glad to be alive. Today, for example, could be a day used as a turning point, the day you decide that enough is more than enough. The fact that you are still alive is cause for celebration. I don't see why not. Since we did not create ourselves, we did not breathe life into our bodies, is all the more reason why we should be so grateful that we are still here. The precious gift of life is no small favor. It's huge. It's the ultimate gift, and we still have it. We've got it! Let's take care of it. Let's show our appreciation and not waste any of the time God gives us. It's His time that we are being allowed to borrow. We would be fools to waste every minutes of our share. Just think, what you choose for yourself today could determine how your future develops. Choose to be wise and wonderful. Be awesome. The Lord God made you brilliant. Show it. You have endured thus far, no more failed expectations. The Lord is your unshakable foundation. With that in mind, start envisioning a better future for yourself. Don't give up and don't give in to negative thoughts. Don't let anything toxic control. If it's not good for you, don't have anything to do with it. You deserve better. Transform your mind to the purpose of the Creator. Your willingness to do better for yourself will bring you days of victory. A great many people lack the desire to go on living because of the feelings of hopelessness that has become so much a part of who they are. The reality is they don't have to suffer. Hope is in every breath that we are given. Any cruel events that might have taken place in your life does not make you a less extraordinary creation, nor does any inner slaughters that you might be living with. You can emerge on higher ground. Brief ecstatic moments are not the only amounts Jehovah have scheduled for you. You are meant to live a spectacular life. You were not born to be a beast of burden in any way, shape or form. Depression is not only disruptive and inconvenient, but it continues to murder the innocent. Depression is just another killer we should never hand our lives over to. Do whatever those positive things are that will keep you from crashing your life all together. The wonderful plans that you had for your life before sadness came calling should not be cast aside forever. Whatever it was that went wrong, don't throw away the rest of your life because of it. Most of us alive in the world today will experience more than one cruel circumstance beyond our control in our lifetime, but we should not let this reality force us to an ending God would not approve. With the positive power of faith on your side, you are capable of great new things. You yourself are a blessing. You are a blend of so many great things. You might not realize it yet, but you are. Your lack of realization does not make that any less true. You were not meant to live your life mindlessly. Reflections should be comforting. They should always serve a useful purpose as useful as the sunlight. Your reflections should not leave you in an element of self-doubt, fear, inner turmoil and the other makings of the monsters that hide in the dark. Don't misunderstand me. It is very important that you never forget the sufferings that took you from better days to living in between sorrows. But you must not let them keep using you. Your mind should be a place that is full of overpowering positive thoughts. In other words, your good thoughts should be so powerful they overpower any negative remembrances. No cruel memory should be given your permission to eliminate the powerful spirit of greatness that you were born with. You can be like the sunshine above the dark clouds. You were given life so that you can shine, not to be left behind. How many times since you were born have you heard, "Time flies away quickly"? And how much attention have you paid to that truth? Don't throw your moments in time away. They are so brief. Live urgently. It's an emergency. We cannot save today for tomorrow. We get one shot at each new day we are blessed to see. Leap into faith. Give yourself permission to dump the dinky little life mentality and start living a life of limitless joy. Give yourself the gift of a better life reach. What I meant by that is, work towards the best life possible. Never get comfortable with the uncomfortable. It is, in my opinion, sinful to make one's own life more difficult than it needs to be. As you also now know, I too was once guilty of such a sin. I almost drowned in sadness. My own experience with the difficulties that come with sadness is why I urge you to do whatever positive thing it takes to move on instead of waiting helplessly for another round. Every survivor of life's cruelties must live with the burden of those memories, but they should not be able to use and abuse your mind. As some of us know all too well, the effects of deep prolonged sadness can be very costly. Depression should not become a part of your character at all. It will never be an accurate match. Be the master of your own mind. Refuse to let anything or anyone own it. You can power out the negatives from their control over your life.

CONTINUING YOUR SURVIVAL

ONE of the rules of your life should be that happiness must be strictly enforced. With positive thinking full of faith, any powerful thing is possible. No matter how tough the times have been for you, you can still go on to serve all of your God-given purposes. Yes you can, and you can do it in spite of the setbacks. Try on happiness for a change. You will love the size of it. Choosing to live a life of happiness should not be a difficulty choice. Happiness is not inaccessible to you, not if you want it bad enough. You only need to want freedom from the inner slaughters. You must believe that you can get to a place of peace while you still have breath. The pity party time is not the invention of Jehovah. It will only work to lower your life. You were not born to live a low life. You were born to live the highest life possible. Long before you and I came into the world, there were people who knew this. There are still people in the world today who know this and gives themselves titles such as Lord, King, Queen, Prince, Princess, and so on. And they expect the rest of us to respect them for it. Clearly they don't see themselves as low-life people, no matter what kinds of emotional difficulties they have to face. They are able to separate any kind of emotional difficulties from the good life they feel they are entitled to. Their way of seeing reality is that of total entitlement. They see themselves as people who are entitled to the very best that life has to offer, and they expect nothing less.

You have Jehovah's permission to be happy, as happy as can be. You are not a peasant. So much belongs to you too. You are also a real Queen, a real King, a real Princess, a real Prince, made by the same powerful loving hands that made those other kings, queens, princes, Lords, princesses and so on. Why should you be considered any less valuable? You have the same entitlements. Why shouldn't you be happy too? Have your say. Have your great, big, powerful, joyful, happiest life. Why not? Why shouldn't you have it God's way? Why should the thief call depression be more intelligent than you? Let nothing here on earth keep you from getting your full blessings. You came from royalty. You came from the original heavenly royal Father. Hold your head up high and walk with confidence upon the earth. You have the ultimate royal blood running through your veins. This is a troubled world. Even so, you can be happy now. You don't have to live in sadness. You can take back control of your life. You are far more powerful than the enemies that lurk in your mind. Doing something positive about the problem of depression is a must if you are to live a better life. You had the strength needed to go through and survived all that you have. That should tell you that you also have the strength to be better than you were before. You have as much inner strength as anyone who is determined not to live a life of failure. Unhappiness does not have to dominate what's left of your life. You can be as successful as you want to be. You do have a powerful, built-in back-up system. It is from this positive power that you can grow to heights no devil can reach. With this power that is centered and anchored in you, all things will work together for good. With that built-in positive power of the supernatural God being harvested even the most vicious of circumstances can be turned to your advantage. You will be so fantastic. The most cold hearted will have no choice but to wish you well. I call that the bearable right attitude. If you can bear the hell that is unfortunately so much a part of the world that we are living in today, you can also bear the wishes of Jehovah for your life. Happiness as it should be is easy to endure. I find it difficult to understand why some people who could and should be happy just flat out refuse to be. Instead of choosing to be happy, they choose instead to spend every waking moment making themselves and everyone else around them miserable. Their words as well as their actions are full of gloom and doom. I now believe that once someone is blessed to have survived and escaped any of life's difficulties, especially the enormous difficulty of physical and emotional abuse that should be cause for celebration. The rest of your life should be spent celebrating your survival, not dragging down what's left of your life with what was. Dump the toxins as best you can, and get on with it. Refuse to do your life in misery. The past should not be used as an excuse to waste your life now. If you are someone who doesn't have to be unhappy, why choose to be? It's not a good choice. There are so many great things that you could be doing with your life instead. Determination should always be used wisely. The saddest place on earth should not be you. Super-size your positive ways. Live in the reality that our days here will never be as many as the earth's. We have seen that fact become even more of a reality for others countless times, yet there are still people living careless, thoughtless lives that without the intervention of love of self will only get worse. Sadness is more than willing to take a controlling place in your life if you let it. You will never receive a gift that is as great as the gift of each new day. Ask anyone like myself who narrowly escaped death more than once. Your life should never be taken for granted. Your entire being should be a wonderful place of peace for you to live. How can any part of your body function the way God intended for it to if your mind is not how it should be. Your mind has great healing power that can not do for your body what it should when depression is present. It's obviously not a good mix. The healing power of the human mind is certainly another cause for celebration. It is one of the blessings you should be celebrating everyday. There is just way too many of us living lives that are being sliced up by daily frustration, anger, sadness, revenge, anxiety. While we busy ourselves with an overdose of these toxic emotions time keeps slipping away from us, and before we know it, a big chunk of our lifetime will be gone, wasted on the unnecessary, so much precious time given away to the useless, toxic emotions that should not have been given the power to represent your humanity in such enormous quantity. Dwelling on a bad past slows your life down in the worst ways possible. I strongly recommend you spend the rest of your life in joyful heavenly bliss. In depression is a terrible way to live the only life that you will ever have. Wise up. Remember you came into this world a free person. Leave it as such. Jehovah knew what He was doing. There are a billion and one reasons why you were born to be free. Give yourself the freedom to live your best life. Don't be gone before your sadness is. Don't put up with anymore nonsense. Please make the most positive use of the precious gift of life you were given that you can. Most people who are living in deep depression don't lack substance. They just don't remember what they did with it. They are too busy being miserable. Having faith in God will result in a great deal of confidence. Suffering the pangs of daily mental anguish is certainly not how you were meant to be welcome into this world. You must try harder to let it be over and done with. Being miserable is not the true meaning of life, not even close. There are great true meanings to life, but that is definitely not one of them. Insist on joy before it's a rap. Find your true happiness place in this world before it's too late. I am not trying to frighten you. We can all use a little more encouragement from time-to-time. That is what I am praying these words; will do for you. Positive reinforcements cannot be too much when our souls are in need of mercy. There are simply too many souls in the world today that are starving for love, understanding, and compassion who don't realize how positively powerful and special they are. Their inner strength is not yet known to them. They still see themselves as nothing. I was one of those starving for love, understanding and compassion people. My soul was almost starved to death, and it showed on my body. Don't starve your soul to death. If you have ever wanted to look at God while He is talking just look at yourself as you take each breath. That's God talking. You don't have to become a mental, emotional, spiritual and physical mess. The life you still have in your body is too valuable and important to waste. Start doing those wonderful things that make life worth living. You have the inner strength that you need to get back on the path that is the place you have every right to be. You can faith your life back into newness and become a source of peaceful knowledge, love and happiness. You can stand for dawning. You can become a welcoming place of comforting knowledge for souls in need of positive reinforcements. Your kind words of comfort could provide a refuge for a lost weary soul. Remove the excuses for staying sad. It accomplishes nothing good. You can actually arrive at such a peaceful place in your own soul that you can become someone who is of great help for the still suffering souls. A sudden force of sadness is able to steal your true character in minutes and if given the power to can hold you for life. It will hang onto your dear life because it keeps you from being of one clear mind. It is quiet difficult to find your best self again if you are drowning in sorrow and refuse to be rescued. Learning to cling to a well deserved life of inner peace and happiness should become the easiest thing in the world for you to do. Your life should not become a drifting along experience. Decide today to start focusing on the things in life that give you hope instead of focusing on the hopeless thoughts that are robbing you of the God-given inner peace that you are still entitled to. Your best hopeful thoughts will help to get you back into the best rhythm of life. There is no way for any human being to benefit from neglect. For example, if you decided to remain in the custody of depression, that would be nothing less than excessive neglect. How you treat yourself says a lot about the condition of your mind, and the things it says to the rest of the world about you are not good either. The gift of life should never be ignored because of anything else. There is not a single gem stone anywhere on this planet that is as valuable as you are. Throwing your life away for the destruction of sadness is an unnecessary cross to bear. You should not have to carry such a burden. In fact, your heaviest dose of daily reality should always include a laughter or two. Handle your life lovingly, especially on those days when you are certain the skies became cloudy because you walked beneath them, and it seems you have nothing left on earth to be thankful for. Go on and do the sun proud anyway. Shine as you give thanks to Jehovah for the gift of your life. Be as thankful as a new rose that burst into bloom at the sight of the sun. Be thankful that you too were included in the greatest miracle. Don't punish yourself for being. As long as you live, you will never receive a gift anymore precious than the gift of life. The first time my mother told me, "Enjoy your life, Sweetheart, before you run out of it," I was in my early twenties. Let's be honest, when some of us are young, the last thing we care about is how quickly time passes, especially when at that very youthful age, we had no intention of ever getting even a day older, even though all around us we could see people of every age, time's story and the evidence of its power over our lives. On a subconscious level, youthful arrogance told us that if you were a very old person, that was your problem, not ours. Some of us were so sure time would not do to us what we saw it doing to others. So why should we be concerned about it? It had nothing to do with us, right? We did not tell them to get older, did we? My mom did not stay in the world as long as I would have liked for her to have, but she did, however, stay long enough to have the experience of being years older. She had no more time to stay here. She is laid to rest in a cemetery in England. What I wouldn't give for one more day with my mom. I will love and miss her for the rest of my life. I sure wouldn't care about her age. Our life is precious no matter how old we are. It should be respected and appreciated. I can tell you from my own experiences with deep sadness that it is an emotion with a big wedge that it has no fear of driving. Another important daily reminder should be that you were created with zero self doubt and that is because you were put together by a great Power who had no doubt about you. Not a single moment of doubt about who you were created to be, you were put together by greatness. Show it. You are an awesome light of life. Treat yourself with kindness instead of with harshness. Never surrender your power to the darkness of evil. You will for as long as your soul survives be a miracle. You are a precious miracle that will stay that way for all eternity. Positive changes should never feel threatening to a miracle. You are a miracle that should have nothing to do with anything less than a joyful existence for the rest of your days. Most of the time the power that we need to make the necessary positive changes in our live is not the kind of power that we need to look outside for. We already have it right there within us. You have the power needed to help remove the poisons from your mind before the end of your life story. You have it within your power to refuse to live in hostile remembrances. Once you decide to put the word "lovingly" into action on your life, your weary body will benefit beautifully from your more conscious mind. You can get your mind to a place so peaceful you will be compelled to give yourself the opportunity to grow from almost any location on earth. One of the ways that I look at a miracle is as the positive at its most maximized. Of course that is also how I see life itself, as the miracle of a positive thought maximized. If you really want to expand your prosperity, there must be a positive change in your attitude towards life. It's as simple as that. Thirsty for change? It cannot come into being without your full cooperation and determination to live a more fulfilling life. Faith itself is full of determination. Let a new season of a full harvest begin with your healing. No one should spend their entire life being a victim. With the right faith filled attitude, you will excel in ways others will envy. A new start as fresh as the early morning dew can be yours. It's time. Don't you think so? You can make a mighty powerful comeback. Life itself is a victory. You have that over depression. You are more powerful than worry. You were made that way. Embrace your gift of life more lovingly. This is an act of faith that will encourage you to keep pursuing a bigger and better life. Having faith that the Creator of life was not mistaken when He gifted you with life will give you the right positive changes you thought would never be yours. You can have many miracles of your own. You don't need to envy anyone. You are good. You are better, and you are also the very best that God has to offer. If you expect to be sad for the rest of your life, then that is how it will be, a self-fulfilling prophecy. However, if you expect and are determined to be the positive filled powerhouse of humanity that you were created to be, that's Jehovah's fulfilling prophecy. It's the only way that it should be. Go on. Rejoice. Lose control joyously as you value your own life. Spoil yourself with laughter. Hurry! Start today. Please start today. As you now know, time will not wait for us. We get such a small amount of it. There is not enough time to laugh as long as we would like to, not enough time to do any of the other things we enjoy doing as long as we would like to keep doing them. We can not afford to keep putting things off. Did you know that you might be the most talented, most gifted one of your generation and don't know it because you have buried your confidence in sadness? No matter how you look at it, living with a heart full of sadness is a very wasteful way to exist. It's a crime being committed against you everyday, the victim and the abuser being one in the same. If that sounds horrible to you, I'm glad it does because it is horribly wrong to spend your time being determined to waste as much of your life as possible. It's time to get rid of any kind of destructive mentality and start healing. Every peace loving human being deserves Jehovah's best. Hold on to faith. Give it the opportunity to take your life to the whole places where you belong. You are a miracle, but without faith in a power greater than yourself. No amount of your effort is enough to bring you the other kinds of miracles that you need now. Trust that having even the tiniest amount of faith can transform and give your life the flying power that it needs. The more you embrace sadness the more overpowering it will become. Without your willingness to help it, a negative past cannot stay alive. At this point in my life, I cannot imagine giving up my power to past cruelties. You are entitled to as much happiness as a king or a queen. Like a leach, these angry toxic emotions turned inward for months or years, that we describe as sadness or deep depression is relying on us to stay alive. The longer we choose to embrace them, the more power over us we are giving to them. I have seen many a life wrecked by depression. Of course because we are human beings, there will be times in our lives when we are knocked down so hard by the unexpected, we are left with feelings of confusion and weakness. It is in those trying times that courage and faith becomes our best anchor. Faith in the power of Jehovah" wisdom is always well worth the benefits, especially in those times when we are ready to accept that there are some things that we cannot do alone. We need divine help for those things that are beyond our control. We deserve to be happy, not only because we are all almost out of time, and when we are gone, we are done forever. We deserve to be happy because we are here now. We exist here on this earth. This is our gift of time to enjoy. We should not worry so much about yesterdays. Those days are dead and gone. No matter how much we cry over their passing, there is nothing that we can do to bring them back to us. There are ways out of sadness. Give faith a try. It is amazing.

The last time I told someone that God will take care of you, it was to a mother whose five year old son had just died, and she was in such emotional pain, I feared she might give up on her own life. She became very angry with me for telling her that God would take care of her. "Where the hell was God when my baby was dying? Why didn't your merciful God take care of my baby?" She asked me with bloodshot eyes and almost foaming at the mouth with anger. A few days later, I saw her again, and she was a much calmer person, but she was still obviously suffering inside. So I said to myself, this might not be such a bad time to speak with her. As I approached her, I was well aware that she could get angry at me all over again, and perhaps ask me, "What the hell do you want this time?" And I told myself that if she did, I would keep in mind that, *a soft answer turns away wrath, but grievous words stir up anger.* The moment that she saw me approaching her, she did her best to smile at me. It was not her most pleasant smile, but I was grateful for it because I wanted to see if I could ease her suffering. During our conversation that lasted almost an hour, I told her that I believe that sometimes God needs to remove a soul from the flesh for reasons that go beyond our understanding. Sometimes a soul is removed to release it from further suffering and/or from the sinful ways of mankind. No matter how brief the time is that we are blessed to get to spend with our loved ones, we have to be grateful for it. In order to keep a soul safe from further violence or to protect many souls from the evil of others, God's will must be done. God does move in mysterious ways. We are a flesh and blood creation. We cannot understand all of the reasons God has for taking a soul back from us before we are ready to let them go, but He does not need our permission to rescue and take back what's His. Before the conversation ended, I decided to remind her of these following words taken from the Bible. "Trust in the Lord with all thine heart, and lean not unto thine own understanding."

There are any number of reasons why someone would suddenly or slowly yield to sadness and remain that way as though it were a natural part of who they are. Nevertheless, there is a way out of this madness that is called sadness. Give faith a try. You will be very pleased with the changes in your heart. Revive and renew your spirit. Do something positively powerful for your life. Don't live your one and only life in a crisis. Why drive yourself crazy leaning unto your own understanding? You are only human like the rest of us. We don't always know why certain things happen. We will never have all the answers to all of our questions, but I promise you that if you will trust the Lord with all of your heart, you will be empowered. People will start to notice the positive changes in you. God will still be there with you, only now you will feel His presence near you. The uncomfortable feelings will leave you. You will know that the power of God is standing by you. Just a single positive thought of faith can be so powerful, powerful enough to lead you to a higher spiritual attainment. As time passes, the deep sadness that became so much a part of your humanity will no longer be a daily problem. Knowing that the love of God is yours to keep forever should be very uplifting to you. In spite of this so-called modern day world that we are living in, *with God all things are still possible*, and will continue to be so. Please believe me when I tell you that the horrible forces of evil are not your master. No unpleasant experience is able to condemn you unless you decide it should be. So don't ignore the fact that you were born blessed. Yes, you! This is true regardless of poverty, ignorance and the false powers with its abusive mentality. You were not born to live weak. The environment that you were born into cannot erase the fact that you were born blessed. You had nothing to do with the type of environment that you were born into. It is not necessary to take the blame for it, feel ashamed because of it, or carry any guilt about it. The childhood environment that you were brought up in, good or bad, was not your doing, nor was it your fault. It was an environment that you found yourself in. That's just how it was. Not every one of us was born into an environment of peace, wisdom and joy. It is very unfortunate that some of us as children found ourselves surrounded by adults who were not wise enough or sane enough to know how to protect the most innocent among them. It's tough to be an adult surrounded by ignorance and a lot tougher still to be a child who is surrounded by adults who are just full of barbaric ideas about life. Realize that you were created blessed. Don't be afraid to let those disturbing old memories pass from your daily life and make room for peaceful new ways. Christ Jesus is with you always. Don't let yourself be used by disturbing old memories. It's the kind of robbery you cannot afford. If you wish for yourself an easier more fulfilling life, start using faith. Start trusting and believing the power that gifted you with life. The precious mighty name of Jesus is always going to get all of heaven's attention. Your precious life does not belong in the wasting draining emotion that is depression. That is not the kinds of transitions that your life needs. No one has ever been sustained by hopelessness. Even someone in the deepest, darkest recess of depression is aware it is not empowering. It is certainly not preserving. From the moment that we take our first breath, a great peaceful, joyful adventure should have begun. It is very unfortunate that this is not the case for many who were born into incomprehensible horrors all across this globe.

Now that you have matured enough to be able to take gentle care of your soul, your mind, your body, why not? Why not give yourself the greatest life that you can? If Jehovah God Himself approved of your happiness, you should not be willing to settle for anything less. To accept that your life is always going to be an unhappy life because of past situations or events that were out of your control is not only offensive to you, it is especially offensive to your Creator. You are better than that. Don't be used by disturbing old memories. It's a robbery you cannot afford. Take better care of your mind. A healthy mind will always be to your benefit. Give back to yourself the stolen peace. Your sweet positive day dreams should not keep slipping back into the horrors you once experienced. Your life while you are still here on earth belongs to you. Don't give those past painful experiences the opportunity and excuses needed to stay in your life. Be loyal to the royal you. Be kind to your own soul and reach for the well deserving beautiful life. Don't let the unpleasantness of the past continue to control you. Make up your mind to be the one and only true earthly master of your life. So many people who have cried long enough and suffer long enough still don't realize that Jehovah's reach is long enough. Make the right decision today to be happy. It will not only increase your survival, the quality of your life will be greatly improved. A wasteful, gloomy existence serves no good purpose. You are a valuable source of will power. If you were blessed with a thousand years of life time here on earth, it would still not be enough time for you to learn all that there is to learn about your own humanity. Knowing that there is so much yet to be learned about yourself, shouldn't you be hurrying to learn as much as you can about you, instead of wasting today looking back on yesterdays? You can only learn more about yourself if you are willing to stop denying yourself the opportunity to do so. In the meantime, it's in your best interest to refuse to compare yourself to anyone else. Like it or not, you will never be anyone else but you. No matter what you do to yourself physically, trying to be someone other than who God made you to be can sometimes descend into madness, causing a big reduction in your natural spiritual strength. It's an attitude that cannot satisfy your soul. Doing all that you can to become someone else is certainly not a healthy way to live your life. Being a truly good person on the inside where it counts is a part of yourself you should not ignore. I have seen people who are so dissatisfied with who they are on the inside that although there was nothing wrong with their bodies, they spent hundreds of thousands of dollars to doctors who were more than willing to cut up their bodies for them in order to change their physical appearance so that they could look like someone else, when all they really needed was an increase in self love, respect and acceptance. I don't want to leave you with the impression that I am against cosmetic surgery. I do understand that sometimes this kind of surgery is very necessary. I am all for someone wanting to look their best, and if surgery is required for physical improvement, sometimes this can be a great thing to have happened. What I am against are the surgeries performed because someone's soul is so heavily burdened with the self-hatred resulting from cruel games of one on helpless one that were played on them before they were capable of defending themselves. That is why they grew up not wanting to look like themselves anymore, believing that if they look like someone else the past will get better or reverse itself all together. You by yourself are a valuable important human being. No one needs to look like someone else in order to have value. No one else in this world carries with them more value as a human being than you do. As you know, you by yourself did not decide to enter into your mother's womb and be born into the world. As you also know, you were placed there. What you look like when you came out of your mother's womb was not up to you. It was not for you to decide. You were made a genuine original. Embrace that truth. Do your best to love yourself just as you are, and leave the rest to Jehovah God. Have faith that He knows just how to fix the past. The heavy price that some of us have been forced to pay for the breaths of life we are given is more than enough. We should not have to live in mental anguish for the rest of our lives. Our Creator wants us to be happy which is why included into our humanity is the ability to create beautiful things. Music, one of my favorite things, is one of those beautiful things. You can make each new day a pleasure filled day unlike no other you have experienced before. You are a magnificent creation that was meant to journey in peace. Would you believe that it was meant for goodness and mercy to follow us all the days of our lives? It's true. Jehovah wants everyday of our lives to be good. You are so important, so valuable, so precious and special that heavenly angels are assigned by God to dwell in your presence for as long as you shall live. This heavenly fact should make you want to cherish your life even more. Please cherish your own life in spite of the fact that your trust in your fellow human being was badly shaken. Hope should never fade from your life, especially not by way of your inaction and dissatisfaction with the outward appearance or with life in general. You may not feel as if you do, nevertheless, you still have enough of the courage it takes to live an even better life after the disappointments. Do the wonderful things it will take to release your mind from the things that left you in shock and disbelief, things that will help you to move forward. Make new friends, the real kinds, not the fake friends. Make as many true friends as you can, and then start forming a peace club. Dance together. Laugh together. Tell jokes. Have a contest to see who can tell the best gut busting jokes. Sing together. Have a contest for that too. Take up a small collection to buy the winner a little reward for their effort. Write your own songs. Form a planet traveler club and travel all over the world with people you love and trust. Learn something new about the earth that we live on. Get a pen and paper and start making notes about the things you love most about life and the world that we live in. Make a list of a hundred or more lovely things that you would like to do before you are not able to. Don't sit around waiting for sadness to rob your sense of independence beyond the point of repair. There are a million lovely things that you can do for yourself that will also show your appreciation for life. I know that not everyone who is sad lacks appreciation for life. Sometimes when we get hit hard by the unexpected, we shut down. We find that the emotional pain is just too much. I understand all too well how that can be. Even the most decent, the most honest human being is entitled to feel anger, but it should not control your life. Use the power of faith as your turning point. Sadness is a dangerous, careless company that should not be keeping you. Immerse yourself in love, peace and joy instead. Don't wait. Begin now, and when you do, expect the extraordinary things that the gift of your loving creation has to offer you. Include yourself back into the celebration of life. Don't forget the best and brightest light here on earth is you. Don't dim your light and set your life back. You have the inner strength to use the power you were given to build within you an empire of faith. Start constructing a peaceful, more powerful way of living. Use your powerful mind to build a system of joy. Yes you can. It is not out of your abilities. You can do it. You are not a weak little baby kitten. You can do whatever you set your powerful mind to. Faith in Jehovah God will help you. Faith is a power that is full of second chances. It can expand you life greatly in all of the right directions. Any unpleasant adjustments that you were forced to make in the past should not be representing you now. You are worth so much more. It's time for you to realize it. After difficulties are over, the experience can be used to our benefit. Looking out for yourself in the right honest ways that will give you lasting benefits is not a sinful thing to do. The truth is, if you are always unhappy, it's very likely that those people who are closest to you will be too. Most people don't like trouble. It is so much better to spread laughter instead of dragging yourself and others down. Why not do the opposite instead? Lift your spirits so high others will want to join you as you soar above all.

Why some of our fellow human beings choose to be a transporter of evil is something the rest of us will never understand. The fact that you are still alive makes you not only a survivor, but a true overcomer. If from this day forward you decide to live your life with a deeper appreciation, I assure you God will crown your efforts with sweet lasting successes. I have found that having faith that there is a Power in the universe that is far greater than that of mankind is very therapeutic. It heightens my chances of being more successful with the things that are important to me. It is a great security force that keeps me from returning to the bitter embrace that sadness once had me locked into. It's the more careful gentle help that my life needs which is why I use it everyday, as plenty full as I can. Having faith that I will continue to be okay is for me the best possible care that I can take of my life. For me, faith is a realistic sustaining heavenly power that benefits every inch of me and helps me to deal with the situations that once had me falling apart. Don't consider it unusual to find out you can realize the same benefits. Your chance at faithing successfully is as good as anyone else's. You can begin to walk with a presence of special extra power that is yours to harvest anywhere at any time. Oh yeah, enduring strong child born from miracles, use your survival to thrive. Have full confidence in the knowledge you do not walk alone.

Hide no more in the shadows that evil dares you to remove yourself from. Permanent victory became yours the moment you were given your precious breath of life. Gift your best self to the living days that are gifted to you. Live with nothing less than your strong, powerful, healthy mind. See yourself in everything fabulous. Make this day a best time for renewing, and remember to live urgently. A little effort on your part is all that is needed to unlock the doors of success that has been closed to you for far too long now. It can be done. Faith is your master key. You don't have to continue embracing sadness. It's a misrepresentation of your humanity. It really is true that most people who have difficulty falling asleep at night and are just not able to get a good night's rest did not get that way because they are too happy. Don't fool yourself and play losing games with your life. You were not born to lose. That should never be the case. You were born a winner. Sadness will cause you to miss out on the most wonderful things in life everyday. Don't lose your best life. Don't throw you away. Please stop now. Your body cannot continue to sustain itself and give you the best results possible if your mind is caged in the wrong thoughts. You were not created from negative thoughts. Try not to use them. They will use you too, in the worst ways imaginable. The damaging effects of toxic emotions to the human body always end up costing a lot more than anyone has ever willingly paid. Blessings that will continue for the rest of your life cannot come to you unless you are ready to receive them. You are a great treasure that should not be living under the domination of depression. The inclusion of long-term grief in your life is not the strong successful life your Creator had in mind for you. There is a way out of the daily assaults. There is a way to the prosperity of lifelong happiness. It is never necessary for any of us to live our lives under the dark clouds of unresolved issues. They will continue to choose for you.

Most adults in the world today understand by now that our minds are far more powerful than we know how to imagine. I must tell you that I truly believe happiness is a necessary element for the human mind if we want to harvest our best lives. Deep rooted sadness, anger, rage and the wickedness that these feelings include is a waste of powerful mind. It truly is. The best gift that you can give to yourself is not the one at Christmas, not the one you buy yourself on your birthday. The best gift that you can ever give to yourself is the gift of inner peace. Believe that having the right kind of faith will lead to your finally having that inner peace your soul has been thirsting for. Trust Jehovah. If you have that very necessary inner peace, the rest will be a whole lot easier. Faith and inner peace is two of the most powerful human soul fuel that there is. Removing the dangerous feeling that can be so addictive from your mind will make room for the kindness to yourself that should always come first. It is very necessary to be kind to yourself in order to harvest and maintain your spiritual strength. The kindest and most loving thing that you can do for you is to release yourself from sadness into the power of faith. If you will do that, you will begin to reap the harvest of goodness and mercy that is intended for your life. You can have the life you once thought would remain an unfulfilled dream. A life of inner peace and the freedom that comes with it can be yours. Faith in a Power greater than yourself and in the power that was placed in every inch of your being before you entered this world is yours to use right at this minute.

The freedom to live a life of inner peace is meant for all of mankind. A life of inner turmoil was certainly not the intended purpose of your life. Now is the time in your journey to learn to recognize the preciousness of your own life. It is my humble opinion that life should be lived for the best of it, which is why in this my precious lightning fast moving days I crave only those things that will enrich my life. I focus on the prosperities of happiness. Let it be the highest on your list of priorities. Refuse to let the inner struggles direct your life. Every time I tell someone that I am working on a special lifetime healing project, they never fail to ask me two things: How? And why? Of course I never drag anyone down with all of the specific details of my most sorrowful childhood days. The details of my bad childhood experiences are not something I like inflicting on others, so I never tell anyone the entire story. I just tell them that I did not have the means to treat myself as well as I deserved to be treated when I was younger. This of course has nothing to do with money. Then I jokingly tell them there is a little girl inside of me who still wants to play. The "How?" question is always easy for me to answer. I explain to them that I do something extra nice, extra special for myself every week day. Then on the weekends I do three extra lovely things for myself on each of those weekend days. I call it my triple blessings days. Those simple acts of gentle, loving kindness has changed how I see myself, changed how I react to the everyday challenges, from the little annoyances to the unexpected, painful, but great lessons. We need something lovely to look forward to, a reason to get out of the bed in the mornings, even if it's just to enjoy a lovely cup of tea or a nice mug of coffee on a cold winter day. Now that I am wiser than I used to be, I am always in search of my greater abilities. I decided years ago to refuse to dwell on those things not intended by Jehovah for my life. In spite of a painful childhood, I know that I was not created under false pretences. My Creator truly intended for me to be here. This, as you know, is a fact for all things given the gift of life. Don't live your life under false pretences. If you are living your life in constant inner sufferings and walking around pretending to be happy, you are indeed living your life under false pretences. You too were created by the most perfectly loving hands. That way, you were made real. Why not live your life as real as you are, as precious as you are? You can stop the pain from devouring your true self. You can have confidence and faith instead of fear. The One who gave you life is your most enduring refuge. You are one of His greatest, one of His finest. He will not refuse you. Our Creator is so much greater than any difficulties that might arise. Trust that your faith in the greatest Power will make the unbearable bearable. It is a faithful, trustworthy power that you can always rely on. There are no risks in this Power, only benefits. These miracle benefits that I am referring to are not rarities. You can feel secure in the fact that miracles are sure to come your way. All you need to do is give faith a try. I am sure that you are able to and can afford to invest some faith in your own life, even if it's no bigger than the size of a mustard seed. Accept that you are loved by the greatest Power that there is. Perhaps you are someone who is saying to yourself, but I am not loved by the person that I want to be loved by. There is a far greater and a lot more satisfying plan for your life. The day you realize it, you will be grateful you did not get those other things you wanted, when you wanted them. I am not telling you these things because I am so grateful for the invention of paper and ink. I am speaking to you from my own experiences, obviously.

There were times in my own life when I directed the insecurities and anger that I was feeling directly at God. I blamed the Creator of my life in a million ways for every single wrong that was ever done to me. At that time in my life, I was still going through the inner hells and confusions. I sometimes saw God as unfair, the great, ultimate Power who did not care enough about the little children of the world. At the same time, I was still going to prayer meetings all over the place. I went to tent meetings, and throughout these prayer services, I kept praying for the miracles I waited. When they did not happen fast enough, I told myself that perhaps God did not love me enough to give those miracles to me. One of my all time favorite preachers is a man from Texas who is now an elderly gentleman. I won't mention him by name because I did not ask his permission to do so. I called him the "no holds barred" preacher. He seemed to me at the time to be a man who fears no devil, something I still love about him. Back then, time had yet to mature me wiser, yet I was so happy to be there listening to him preach, mainly because in those hours, I could forget about the past instead of driving myself crazy with toxic remembrances. As I listened to this great man of God, I had no idea at the time how much I was being taught and being taught the right way. I also had no idea what my tomorrows would bring or the types of investments I was making in the tomorrows I was not yet able to see.

Back then there were times when looking back on the unfairness of my formative years made me so angry I would go to sleep loaded up with disappointments, asking God, "Why?" I lived in grief up to my eyeballs, wondering why this loving God did not grant me the mercy I needed when I needed it most in my life. Why, I wondered, didn't Jehovah God step in and smash the hands of the wicked who dared to brutalize a child? If He has the whole world in His hands, why doesn't He do something to help the little innocent children in His hands? I woke up with those thoughts in my mind almost everyday. That is why after I fell asleep at night, my dreams were not safe from my troubled mind. At that time, I should have been having dreams that force me to wake up laughing every time, not just every once in a while. Unfortunately for me, with each passing year, I was realizing more and more how unfair my childhood was which lead me to ask God more and more questions about the unfairness in the world.

Why the sufferings, especially the little innocent children? What did they do to deserve any of it? What could any little innocent child do to deserve being beaten, raped, starved, to be punished in such incomprehensible ways than there are numbers to count ways? You'd better believe I was angry with God. Of course, since those bitter days, as I mentioned earlier, I have learned that human selfishness, ignorance, and the God-given gift of freewill, that to date is still being abused, are the root cause of most of our problems. There is no question about it. We are the ones who are causing the most difficult problems that we face in the world today. We are the enemy, not little green men from some other far away planet with eyeballs that take up half of the space on their faces. It is us, human beings who consider ourselves to be superior, intelligent beings who know better than the Creator of life how best to do life. I often time wonder how any human being alive today who has seen these mysterious signs and wonders happen right here on this planet right now, such as crop circles, for example, that are begging for our attention, and yet still continue to do evil things. I call those crop circles the "big flags from heaven" because in my opinion, they are some of the most obvious warning signs, those of us alive today have ever been blessed to receive. I believe we should not miss any of our knick of time moments. We can not afford to blow any more blessings. Live beautifully. Live wonderfully. Live with passion. Live as though tomorrow will never come. I spent more than twenty years of my life in deep sadness which as you might understand is not a loud, screaming kind of anger. I lived with a quiet rage that almost cost me my life before faith brought me out of the depths of sorrow. I was also quite angry with God about the unanswered prayers that I prayed during long days of fasting without so much as a tablespoon of water. I could feel my body dying, but I was determined to reach God by whatever means necessary, and I was sure that long fasting and praying for up to nine days at a stretch was one of the best ways to get God's attention. I don't recommend it. Nine days of fasting was an insane act on my part, and most of those prayers that I prayed were not answered at that time. I later had to go back down on my knees without fasting and give Jehovah God thanks for not answering those prayers and begged forgiveness for my unintentional arrogance in thinking I knew best what every road of my life's journey should be on. To this very day I am still grateful and giving thanks to the Almighty that some of those roads that I chose for myself were blocked off in the knick of time. In God's own way, the prayers I prayed during those long fasting days were answered after all, just not in the ways that I as a human being expected them to. God had powerful things planned for my life, things I could not have imagined. He moved in my life in the most mysterious of ways. Those prayers that I prayed from a body that hungered and thirsted did move God. He answered those prayers before the requests left my heart and onto my lips, but I could not see the results of them. All I saw were my own feelings of disappointment. God had me covered, but I felt lost because the results of God's answer to my prayers were not immediate. The tiny scrap of faith that I had left was enough to bless my life and help me to understand that my worth and value as a human being is completely separate from the deep emotional anguish that was brought to bear. As you read this, I invite you to do everything within your power to understand and embrace the truth that what defines you as a person is not the ugly lies you were taught about who you are. Please know this, no other human being here on earth can decide for Jehovah God what beauty should be. Don't allow the shallow thinking from narrow minds to effect how you see yourself. One of the worst things that you can do to yourself while you are still alive in this world is to let the twisted mentality of others cause you to hate yourself. The fact that you were created in the image of the most perfect, the most beautiful love makes you nothing less. Please come to the realization that no one who deliberately does harm to an innocent fellow human being is all about love. The past does not have to keep harming you. Refuse to believe the lies. Provide no lurking room, not even at the back of your mind. Your mind should never become a haven for thieves of any kind. You are the one who was hurt. Why should you have to continue living in a prison of the mind? You are not the one who should be locked up. You don't deserve any more hell. Don't lock yourself away. You possess the positive power necessary to release yourself from the pain and elude capture for the rest of your life. It is perfectly okay to open up your life to showers of blessings. You can start right now harvesting the peaceful inner freedom that is necessary to get on with the rest of your life. There is a big life's harvest yet to be reaped by the suffering souls among us. You can remove yourself from that number and start reaping by faith. Change the negative thinking. It's an enemy. Pray it out and as you do remember that the name of Jesus gets heaven's attention. No decent person should ever allow the cruelness of others to overshadow the miracle of each new day. You will never feel totally secure, happy and comfortable in your own life until you decide and get serious about removing the emotional muck that does not belong on your life. It does not belong on you. Get rid of it! The internal energy that is required to stay depressed is only part of the destruction of a depressed person's life. There are countless other ways that it robs you. I have found that sadness, no matter how brief it lasts, is only useful in the destruction of self. Sadness is a radical emotion that always makes the best of its freedom. You are entitled to a more powerful freedom than sadness is given. It is worth mentioning again that your life is meant to be cradled in goodness and in mercy all the days of your life. The solution to some of our problems that we spend billions of dollars trying to solve would be easily solved if we just change our way of thinking, from negative to positive. Some of you won't believe that, but before you judge me too harshly, keep in mind that I said "some" of our problems, not all of our problems. Changing a hardcore, evil barbarian is another matter all together. That's a job for Jehovah Himself. What I am referring to is the fact that we would need to take less pills if we weren't so sad and stressed out all the time. We need more peace of mind, a lot more love and a lot less pills. Loving and respecting yourself are not only high motivators, but they are also the best ways to give thanks to your Life-giver and reap the great, big benefits at the same time. Please believe me when I tell you that toxic emotions are not ones deserving of your time. I have met people who like myself suffered abuse at the hands of another while they were still at a helpless age, tells me that the sadness they feel everyday as a result won't leave them. Unfortunately, if you are one of those people still waiting for the negative effects of an abusive childhood to leave you, you will be sad to your last day. The unpleasant memories and the horrible depression that often result will never volunteer to leave you. You have to make a conscious decision to leave it. You must go your separate way. The power of positive thinking is a great way to evolve. Make a conscious decision to be a survivor forever. Don't give up now. Fight sadness as the enemy that it is. Whatever makes you sad is obviously not good for you in any way, shape or form. You are an enduring child of a powerful life giving Force, but you do not have to keep enduring so much for so long. I do understand that some emotional wounds are so deep it leaves you feeling hopeless, which in turn can sometimes make it a lot more difficult to hope. Hope is the very thing faith will give you plenty of. A good start up always takes some effort. Your life can be raised up again. I have no doubt about that, and you shouldn't either. I am another living proof that it is possible. If you will just trust that the Giver of life placed you here with a great purpose, the significant growth you will experience will astound you. Require of yourself what's necessary for your total and complete emotional healing. You cannot have the truest, happiest life that you can until you do. Among the healthy things that you can do is stop disappointing yourself. That one thing alone would be a great start up effort. There is a big difference in living each day that you are blessed to be given as though it were your last day here on earth, than living your life as if here on earth you have everlasting days. The world around us is changing so fast. Children grow as rapidly as weeds in the spring season. Should Jehovah continue to lend you days, it won't be long now before you look at the world and wonder where the world you knew went. Make these ever fast moving days your good news days. Don't wait for happiness to find you. Use the guiding light of faith to guide you to it. Oh yes you can! You can start seeing life as a feast that must include positive thoughts to help you get to the best of it. I promise you that a positive attitude will always work to your blessings. If you would decide today to never again make any kind of contribution that could lessen your life, that built-in awesome brain power you did not know you possessed would start coming alive. As you know, most plants need the light and warmth of the sun in order to bloom and thrive in the necessary ways. Your soul needs peace in order for you to thrive in the right ways. If you have the necessary inner peace, you can flourish in ways you never thought possible. It is important to include in your daily reminder the following facts. Please remember that the grip of sadness has real severe costs. It is definitely not a wellness spring. Its effects can pile up rapidly and produce devastating results. These thought did not come from a board guessing game. They came from first hand flesh and blood human experiences. Years of sadness can have the same effect on the human body as deadly chemicals. One of the things sadness does is bury your true disposition obviously. And even though you might not realize it, its effects will be magnified on your face forcing you to stand out in a crowd whether you like it or not. People will notice how sad you look all the time and do their best to avoid your company. If you want to stay here on earth and open the doors of heaven in your favor, be more determined to be happy. Without question, this attitude will draw the right people into your life. You don't want to spend the rest of your life drawing pitiful stares from the strangers who are not brave enough to approach you and offer help. Invest in happiness. Help yourself. Pain should not be camping out in you. By the time most of us are eight years old we are aware we did not create ourselves. Yet not enough of us adults live conscious of the truth our life was given as a precious gift deserving of treasuring. Shouldn't the maximum precious gift of life bring us maximum joy? Was that not the whole idea of our creation? Shouldn't our earthly life's journey be a journey of countless joys? Desire more of the happiness that makes life worth living.

Yes it is true that for some of us, lines were crossed that should not have been. There were horrible acts against our humanity, and yes, we cannot go back and change those cruel acts that weakened us for a time, but it does not have to destroy you. The one reversing that you are still able to do is make a U-turn and go back to your life the way it should be. You can have positive power-filled days for the rest of your days. You can prosper in undreamed of ways. As you journey through, see life as one big classroom. And if you are willing to enroll yourself back into it the way you should be, take your rightful place, and while you're at it, choose to major in joy. You can have a huge future. An abundance of joy can be yours. Don't give any more permission to cruel circumstance to intimidate you. Consciousness can be very scary if you don't know how powerful you are. That is as solid as a rock. How do you use it? First you must cut the pain away from the face of the rock. Start using the power of faith to your advantage. Speak the mighty name of Jesus and fear not. Trust that there is nothing that the forces of hell can throw at you that the forces of heaven cannot handle.

If that day ever comes when I decide to tell the world my life's story thus far, talking about the things I had to overcome, it would take at least five books to tell it all. Desire to use the positive power in you. Achieve the kinds of greatness only the biggest Thinker who gave you that power knew you could. A fragmented life is not the desire of any sane person's heart. It is certainly not what your Creator desires for you. Wasting precious time dwelling on the past can work to feed the negative forces, especially if it is a truly horrible past. You should rebel against evil forces instead of inviting them to dwell in your midst. Those old painful memories will contaminate your life and continue to do so unless you make it stop. It is not impossible to do. It does matter how you live. Regardless of how long you have been allowing those painful memories to take advantage of you, you can still make them stop controlling your life. Most people I know don't like anything bitter. If you appear to be someone who is bitter, that is more than enough to put most people off. This next thing might seem harsh, but it does not make it any less true. There are people out there in the world who will hate you just for appearing to be a person who is bitter. An innocent person who looks bitter can also look like a trouble-maker to some people who were themselves victims of an abusive deviant with a similar body language. That is a killer cycle that you no longer have to be a part of. You can force those years of trauma to fade back into the past where they belong. Past unfairness should not be holding your life hostage. That is not right for you. It is not how you should be living your life. It is safe to say that is not the direction the Creator of your life would point you in. Drenching one's self in bitter emotions would never be approved by any sane person. No decent, innocent human being should ever have to pay for the crimes committed against them for the rest of their lives. Handing over the rest of your life to grief is in itself a crime against your entire being. You can get to win a million times more than you expected to. I said that to you because I have proven for myself on more than one terrifying occasion that when you let the miraculous powers that are yours to use take control and influence your thinking, your strong mind will be restored. You are a seed from the one and only original Tree of life. You are second to none. You are as good as it gets. You are a miraculous power given flesh. You are heaven sent. You were made to showcase joy. Without question, you are the ultimate miracle. You were built to hold joy naturally. Why do you think laughing feels so good to you? It does matter how long it's been since you've had a good laugh, but no matter how long it's been since you did, I am sure you must have some memory of how very delicious it was when you did. You will never be happy if you choose to journey through your human experience as though you are an empty vessel. Unfortunately, there are people who did nothing to deserve hatred, yet they hate themselves. Pain is given regular access to their lives. You and I have witnessed bad behavior by fellow human beings that disturbed us to the core of our being. I have seen drivers on the roads behaving badly. Threatening other drivers become for them, a set standard of daily madness. The intense feelings they are lacking control of is enough to blow up their entire life. Obviously, this kind of out of control behavior becomes the norm when the human mind is no longer peaceful. Having a cloudy view of your own life is certainly not a way to set a standard of excellence for yourself as an adult. Next to the Creator, you are the most important influence in your life. The evidence of our flawed humanity is all around us. Some of us are more flawed than others. My own experience with acts of violence committed against me makes that fact even more obvious to me. It's fair to say that even more tragic are the lives that become stagnant as the result of a flawed fellow human being. Many years after surviving abuse, many of the survivors still find it difficult to enter into each new day peacefully. For them, being miserable has become the norm. In case you are a person who is having a difficult time enjoying your life as much as you should, I honestly believe that it would be well worth your time to highlight the following. The power of demons and monsters pales in comparison to yours. Now I must ask you for a favor for yourself. Say it out loud. Say it clearly. Say it because you believe that it is true. The power of demons and monsters pales in comparison to me. Shout it loud enough for the demons and monsters to hear you. Don't be afraid. Let them fear you instead. Say it until this knowledge flows into every fiber of your being. The power of demons and monster pales in comparison to me. Say it everyday. You are the natural nature of the Creator. Do you have any idea how big and powerful you can be against demons and monsters? Do you know the kinds of positive power you were given from the beginning? We are the only life form on earth that I know of that can pray to the Almighty. Why not take advantage of the opportunity? You don't have to live emotionally weak and scared half to death all the time. If you are living that way, it is not because God asked you to. That is not the nature of God. That is not how it was meant for you to spend your days. You were not meant to live far from the victory that you are. In the event I just confused you, let me put it to you another way. I believe that when we were successfully created, given the breath of life, that magnificent work of art called human kind was right there at the top of the Creator's greatest victory. I sometimes wonder how pleased He is with us now. Nevertheless, you are what victory is. I still believe as I did when I was a child that there are a billion more things about the human body we have yet to discover. It is very possible we possess the ability to grow new limbs using God-given powers of our mind. We just have not been able to figure out how to do it exactly. I believe Jehovah God packed more positive power in us than we know. It is also my opinion that part of the reason we still do not know enough about the powers of our Creator is because we are too busy being bad and doubtful. The one thing of which I have no doubt is this. Using one's body as a channel in which through emotional pain can travel on a daily basis should never be allowed. Daily is way too frequent. You are a great source in which only joy should have daily access. Set a standard of excellence for your mind. Be amazed by your own beauty. You have much inner beauty. Open your life to rich newness. Don't waste your loveliness. Locking yourself in a permanent embrace of despair will leave you stumbling in the dark instead of flying in the light of newness as you are meant to. Freedom to enjoy life fully is an entitlement not enough of us take advantage of. Giving the effects of evil the chance to follow you for the rest of your life is a torment that can force anyone to lose sight of the importance of your life. Time not only flies when we are having fun; it passes just a quickly when we are not having fun. Everyday that we are blessed to see is our life time happening. If sadness is holding back your life, it's time to use the positive power in you to break free. Change any unfair negative way that you see yourself. You have the strength needed to clear the path to a brand new life. You may not feel as if you have the inner strength to do what is in your best interest, but trust Jehovah. You do. You should be able to taste the richness of your humanity in every breath that you take. Your soul and mind needs a restful, peaceful body in which to reside. Become that safer place. Don't waste any of the rich positive newness that is yours to experience. Don't waste a single new day. Courage a few of the positive words that should be framed in your mind. Refuse to be held back. A spiritual death, in my opinion, is the worst kind of death. While you have breath, while you are still able to, why not live your sweetest life? You are a sensational creation. You were created with joy unspeakable and filled with the glory of God. The human spirit, when harvested in its intensity and used in the right ways, is still a beautiful thing to behold. We are the greatest life form on the face of the earth. Wipe the sadness from your face. You name too is on that greatness. How do I know that for sure? It's because you were made that way. No devil can keep Jehovah's children from being over comers. If you so choose, past difficulties cannot stomp you down. Desire more of Jehovah's truths. Desire your most successful life. Why not put your life back on the path that is best for your soul? Your spirit will soar with the richness of your positive newness. Rest assured—God has a great voice that is full of powerful wise reasons why we should embrace the opportunity of life that we are given. Why reduce your existence to unnecessary suffering when you know in your heart you can do a whole lot better for yourself? God is our best hope in finding the solutions that we so desperately need. If you were to look around you with an honest and willing heart, you will find under God's heaven the reasons to move on to a wiser way of living. The suffering that depression brings is not your destiny—of this I am certain. Depression is an enormous reduction in self. What is the greatest good that you yourself can contribute as you journey through this life is a question for all of mankind to answer honestly and act upon it. I believe that each and every one of us has something positive that we can contribute if we choose to do so. I promise you that living within the spirit of Godliness will never confine you to the hindrance of darkness. A good healthy mind is a well being none of us can afford to be without. Heaven now does not have to be by way of farewell, but instead, by way of a healthy new beginning. The very concept of you was born from reason. There is a powerfully positive reason for your existence. You cannot remind yourself of that enough. What if you decided today to do that positive thing you've always wanted to do and found out to your amazement that it really is who you are? How sweet it would be for you if you allowed yourself to be free from the bondage of worry. I wish you would. The greatest love that there will ever be is still being proven in every living thing. Give yourself a new rightful start. Make a rich new commitment to yourself. Make up your mind to have inner peace so that you can start enjoying your life even more. Oh thou priceless one. Lose not thyself to woe. Invest in faith. It will provide for you an endless supply of courage. You are the destination of greatness. Greatness does not get any better than you. There is nothing on this earth more precious than a life. I say to you again. Endless wisdom is yours to gain. Don't start worrying about the wasted years past or about the joys you should have had, but missed out on. That is in the past. What's done is done. Be the joy that you still have now. You are the best joy that you do have now. Cherish the life you still have. You are still very much alive. This gift that is today is what matters most. You can make the adjustment from sorrow to joy. Perhaps like myself and too many others in this world, you've gotten to a place of misery because someone had a selfish evil game plan for your life. Make them lose by showing them the winner in you. Take back your life, and run like a healing river of living waters with it. Show them that the power of demons and monsters pales in comparison to yours. Put yourself back into the center of your miracles. They are your miracles. Claim them. Don't be satisfied with anything less than that. It is not right that you should settle for less when you deserve so much more. The power of your faith in the almighty will push those dark clouds away and out of your life forever. I do understand that living in today's world is not easy. Things can get pretty trying at times. Some people have it more difficult than others—no question about that. Even so, don't give up. You are not far from victory. You have it right there with you. Start amazing yourself with the power of positive thinking. Don't steal from yourself. That must always have natural spiritual connection to the Creator. You have a natural chemistry with your Creator. Don't ignore that. You are light, not darkness. Remember with every breath that you take, you are a creation of the most High. No one should be reckless with their life. It's beyond foolish. Your greatest discoveries and your recovery are in the power of faith. Use faith with the same new sense of urgency that you will be living your life with now. When it comes to your own well being, you can be a much higher achiever than you think. Of course, you can. Don't doubt that. Have faith. Your very first breath was in preparation for the greatest time that is your life. You were meant to live in the peaceful, graceful beauty of the earth that was prepared in advance for your arrival. Allowing faith to lead the way will get you those vital victories that you need. Oh how glorious it is for the wise to realize the value in second chances. Living between anger and heartache is so tiring. It's no wonder one is left without the energy or desire to get on with life. After all, sadness does put one out of sync with all that is required to harvest inner strength. You can get your life back to that best place. You are not living alone on some other planet. The suffering does not have to continue. You can make yourself the best positive challenge you have ever given to yourself. You can be your own voice of reason instead of suffering indefinitely. Wounded souls are healed everyday. You can be one of them. You can be filled with hope. It does exist in great amounts. There are a billion reasons for optimism. You have a huge life still waiting for you. Your suffering can come to its ending at last. It is an undisputable fact that depression is a seriously bad state of mind for anyone to be in. This deep sadness that demands so much has caused many people to miss out on what would have been a great life. Perhaps like so many others, you too were taught to lose sight of how truly special and important you are, and still are finding it difficult to believe in the power of positive thinking. Should that be the case, you need to ask yourself, "Has depression worked as a life enhancer for me?" We both know it has not—it never will. Now that you are an adult, it is important to keep in mind that the one and only earthly being that can love you best is you. Treat yourself gently.

No one else walking on the face of the earth today can love you and take care of you in the powerful spiritual ways that you can. When things become difficult for you mentally, only you know beyond a shadow of a doubt what's truly going on with you. Only you know best what you need to have peace and whatever that is. Faith will fly you. What I mean by that is what I told you earlier. You can rise above it. Whatever your inner suffering is about, you can rise above it. Yes you can. You will laugh as much as you should be. No matter how deep the emotional wound is, you do have the strength to survive it. You will survive well beyond today. You are not powerless. It's just how pain makes us feel. Fight with the power of faith, even when it hurts so much you feel you can't go on. Faith in the power of the almighty is a wonderful carver. It will carve you a great new beginning. Treasure thyself. You were not created from negative words. Refuse to continue using them on yourself. Don't let them take root in you. Choose to live without self-condemnation. Look at yourself in a positive way instead. Precious energy should never be wasted on negative thoughts or actions. Taking daily inventory on past mistakes as an excuse to abuse yourself is a sinful way to welcome the sun. There is already too much wickedness happening under God's heavens. Carrying heavy burdens of guilt and feelings of condemnation when you don't deserve them will block your blessing and make it that much more difficult to get back on the road to spiritual freedom and the fulfillment of your best life. Don't choose to continue sitting in the darkness. Demand of yourself the freedom to live in the true heavenly light that you are. We are all far stronger spiritually than we have allowed ourselves to be. Don't give sadness the opportunity to lay you out. Time will do that to us all too soon. No God fearing person should spend every day of their life squeezed between agonies. The days that we are given were not meant to be crushed by distress. Swapping one's happiness for horrors when you have the power to avoid it is not only reckless. It reeks of self-hatred. The rise of a beautiful, peaceful new life should be welcomed. If you are living in deep sadness, you cannot afford to sit tight. Use faith to order the release of the beauty within. End the internal exile and rebuild your life with all of the long term benefits. You were made with long-term value, a guarantee from Jehovah. Your truest self is within your spirit as much as you are in God's favor and grace. You were created to be mighty upon this land, even in times of trouble. Feed to your soul the true promises of God that it needs to thrive. Our heavenly Father will reward your trust in Him. It is because you have survived why you should get up each morning saying, "My newer more positive life is here to stay." You will be pleasantly surprised how many angels will take those positive filled words straight to heaven as it is being made so. As far as we know, we only get this one chance to do life here. Our one chance to do it well, we at least can be certain that we only come along once in this lifetime that we are living now. We also know that life's stage has billions of performers. How are you performing? If you have been waiting for a heavenly inspiration, look no further than yourself. You came here in celebration of glory. You are a note in heavenly music. Let yourself dance while you still can. There are, as you know, many different life forms covering this planet. Even so, I consider us humans the bonus coverage. There are more than a few animals that would not agree with that, I am sure. Nevertheless, I think it is unfortunate that so many of us don't see ourselves as the great miracle that we are. We are truly the greatest miracle walking the earth. Anyone with a sound knowledge able mind knows that in order to count to six billion using one digit at a time, you would have to start with one and count your way up. You could not skip the number one and still expect to have six billion. You would be one number less than six billion. You are only one person out of six billion plus people. Yet you are just as important as the rest. You are just as valuable, just as precious to God. The only way any selfish, evil person can continue to trivialize your life is if you yourself continue to give them the opportunity they need to do so. Remind hell everyday that this is your passage in time. Don't energize the negative events by feeding them the emotions they need to continue stomping you down. You are a source of valuable light that the world needs. You were not sent here because you have zero value. You are far more valuable than you know. You alone can contribute a hundred years or more of greatness. Millions of souls whose passage came to a close before those of us alive today came into the world, made wonderful contributions (too many to list here) that you and I are still benefiting from today, hundreds of years after they left. God sent them ahead of us to make those contributions that he knew we would need when we got here. What kinds of positive contributions can you make to the circle of life? There was a time in my adult life, before I emerged to full positive newness, when I allowed diseased thinkers to plant their toxic waste beliefs in my already too crowded with negative remembrances mind. Back then, if I did not know how to pray, I might have lived everyday according to the lies I was told about my true purpose in this life. That little bit of faith that I had was what saved me from destruction. Sadness will continue to raise its already too high cost if you are willing to remain captured. Living under the controls of sadness creates more than a little disturbance. Some people will never accept the fact that they do not have the right to hurt themselves. We are the property of our Creator, a temple displaying a mighty power. Most people who deliberately do harm to themselves because of self-hatred are convinced it's okay to do so since they are not hurting anyone else. Yet it is a direct assault on our Creator. You did not elect or select yourself. Therefore you do not have the right to reject yourself. You were not made a human vacuum then placed here on this earth to suck up emotional garbage. A mind full of garbage is not your true inheritance. A provision was made for you before your arrival. Garbage is not a part of it. A powerful provision of joy was made for you when you were only a thought. You are not a joke. Don't allow anyone or anything to steal your provision. Don't let it happen. Fair is fair. You came to this earth at this time to take happiness to a new level, to showcase it in ways that have never been seen before. Develop positive unique ways to joy yourself. Take full advantage of your gift of life. Move faster to a new better way of doing life. You have the courage and power to succeed and seal your happiness. Please try to understand why it is so urgent for you to get out of life the happiness that you can get out of it now. Don't forget that you are representing the Creator of miracles. You must get on with the business of living a peacefully rich life. What would life for us be like without music? A life without happiness is a life in decay. I am sure I did not shock you by saying that most people who are depressed know it's not good for them, but they believe they are not strong enough to overcome it. The Almighty is strong enough. With the awesome power of faith on your side, you can find your way out of the deep darkness of depression. Your life can be as wonderful as you hope it will be. You are wiser than you are willing to admit. Don't go through life as one of the myopic people. The Almighty is the same old fashioned, awesome Power that is included in your make up. Yes you, you were made that way—no doubt about it. You are a beautiful reality. Every ounce of God's love was poured into your creation. Love is what you are. It's what you were made from. It's the heavenly power that you are, a wonderful force of positive energy. So much wonderful work was done on you. You are what greatness is made of. You are and will always be the unmistakable evidence of miracles. Prove it to yourself. It is not God that we have to convince. Our Creator already knows how special each and every one of us is. It is up to you now as an able adult to treat yourself as the irreplaceable miracle that you are. Feel more alive. Don't be satisfied until you do. No matter whose big muscles were flexed unfairly on your life, the power that rules the universe has bigger muscles on permanently strong, loving arms. You are being held in love, a love that will never be denied you—come what may. Faith in the Master of the universe and the huge miracles it has drawn has already changed the minds of millions. It is just not worth your time to live your life as though you were created to be evil's stocking stuffer. You are not being held against your will in some sack that you are only allowed to get out of once each year to enjoy a few minutes of sunlight. If that is a similar description of what your life is today, that's all the more reason why you should put an end to the seasons of cruelties. The foods that you eat will taste a lot better to you. There will be a tremendous positive difference in all areas of your life. The loving gift of life is the best maximized that there is. Yours should not be minimized by anyone, especially not by you. There is no replacement for the success of the gift of life. We are so blessed to have received it. Don't limit your success. Your sense of belonging does not have to be lost to you forever. Jehovah's love is full of the right kinds of nourishment that your soul hungers and thirsts for. When you know how truly powerful and special you are, how much you are valued by your Creator, it makes robbing your confidence impossible. You are what happened when positive thoughts joined forces with the power of faith. Those two powerful forces will always be yours to use. You will love the embedded effects of them. There is nothing available to you that is more powerful than the natural heavenly ingredients you were made from. Depend on these powers to provide you with a more stable life. Faith in Jehovah can do so much for you. Before you become too weary of life, remember this. No one else here on this earth can make you as happy as you can make yourself. You don't need any abusive deviant standing over you to convince you of that. You are the stuff of greatness, which is the main reason inner peace is the one merciful must have you should not be living without. There are more than a million reasons why inner peace must be enforced. It is the happier place you should never leave. Inner peace is very much the living waters that your soul needs plenty of. We should not only provide it for ourselves, but we should encourage others around us to do the same for themselves. It is very unfortunate that so many of us have turned a blind eye to the beauty that is life itself. While we are still in transit towards the extending welcoming arms of God, the gift of our lives should always be respected and cherished. Regardless of your age, you should still be defending your life against the fast aging agents that are ever present in toxic emotions. Every single day that you are blessed to be alive presents to you a great opportunity to do something lovely for yourself. Celebrate the greatness that you are. Never forget how lovely things should be for you. Having fun with your life, smiling, laughing, dancing, golfing, fishing, planting a lovely vegetable or flower garden, singing, going for long rides out into the country sides. All of these and the millions of other wonderful life experiences available to you should not be missed. If you can afford to, those trips you have been dreaming about should not be put on hold any longer. Life without happiness is meaningless. Your life has meaning. Don't miss it. The bondage of depression is truly a tiring over-extension of self. If you must over extend yourself, that is certainly not the way to do it. You are one of Jehovah's most important gifts. Protect your interest. I don't think anyone—no matter how bad they are—really wants to suffer. Most people that I know don't want to live a life that includes hellish difficulties. Yet, many of us allow ourselves to continue reliving and renewing a difficult past long after regaining our freedom from the experience. It is very tragic that the evil polluted words of the devil's servants should have such haunting powers over our lives when we do have within us the positive power needed to end the haunting. Way too many of us give second chances to evil. Evil works should never be given the opportunity to haunt us forever. They should not be given permanent residency in our minds. Only the gift of wise words should influence you. In my opinion, it is truly a sin to set aside the true purpose of your life in order to concentrate on being defeated. Whose bad influences might you be living under? One of the most powerful things that you can do for yourself right now is rise up into the positive force that you are. Harvest every ounce of positive power that you were given by the Almighty and show the enemies what you are made of. Don't lie down like a dog licking its wounds. Stand up and fight for your life. Grow upward in the power of faith and make them stand down. There are people out there in the world who will use you if they get the impression that you are a weak person who lacks faith and confidence. Living your life with a defeated mindset only causes more internal rifts. Living with a sad mind interferes with God's special plan for your life, whether or not you intended for it to happen. Because your existence represents the greatest loving, active power in the universe is why you are already in possession of all that you need for a more fulfilling life. If you must survey the damage again, do it one last time, then put a powerful mustard seed amount of faith right into the other actions needed to start repairing your life. The Almighty can cast a wider net than any that He has given the gift of life to. It must be said that any failures during the hardest hit of realities is certainly not always an invited fault of ours. We are, after all, only human. Blessedly, we can use faith to create the conditions that will allow the broken pieces left to be put back together by the One who knows best how to. You will find that the safest and absolute best environment for the human soul is a peaceful one. For those of us who have withstood the cruelest test of time, gifting ourselves with an environment of peace is a must, always. Don't wait for worse things to convince you of that. Start making the most of every breath that you take. Realize how breathtakingly beautiful you are. Take your life back from the tormenting so that you can find the peace necessary to move on. Start enjoying more the natural beauty that is you. Use your access to the ultimate power then unveil a brand new life. You deserve a beautiful, peacefully rich life. This day, this time in human history is your place, your moment. You can still seize the opportunity. You can still have a stunningly beautiful life. Painful events have certainly dragged some of us across extremes and changed the equation of our lives. Be that as it may, none of the unfairness applies should remove the necessary attention you need to pay to your own life. Without the benefit of good mental health, none of us can function at a hundred percent. Spending the rest of your life being a victim is not a cluster any of us can afford. What you have to offer yourself should be healthy offerings on every level. Dazzle the world with your brilliance. Be more dedicated to your happiness. We were created to be powerfully good. It is the right destiny too many of us fall short of. Refuse to put your life on hold indefinitely. It is simply not fair to live a lesser life than you deserve. No one should live their entire life believing that someone else's value as a human being far outweighs their own. You are a chosen, marvelous creation of the greatest Supporter that there is. You are one of the living results of faith. Let that big light of your shine. You should be reaping the full benefits. Misery is just as plentiful as happiness is. Which ever one you offer a way to enter into your life to take up residency will do so. It is up to you now to choose wisely. Living a life that does not include mental health assaults may seem unattainable for someone who was raised in an environment of antagonism and/or senseless violence. I can assure you that this unfortunate restless start does not have to go the full length of your precious life. The rest of your life does not have to play out in the same negative examples set for you in your formative years. Be more determined to see to your own happiness. Your life should not continue being eroded by memories that should be no more than toxic waste. You are entrusted to the earth and to our fellow human beings. The evil done by mankind is no fault of yours any more than it is the fault of Jehovah. Create your own happiness in your little corner of the world. You will never be forgotten by the loving source that gave you so much beauty. Live in the memory that you are a blood relation of the greatest Source of miracles that there is. You stand to benefit greatly. Putting yourself together with the positive power of faith is a very necessary togetherness that will keep you the winner you were created to be. Neglecting your own life is a gross mismanagement of such a precious gift. It is to all our benefit to keep in mind that even faith not bigger than that of a mustard seed gives nothing less than a large return, especially in those times when the things we pray for does not come to us at the time we prayed that it would. To reap an entire harvest takes a little more time. If you are using the right method to do so, you have only to wait upon the Lord. Getting the best as well as getting the most of your rightful life time inheritance will take patience on your part. We would be wise to always remember that. True faith is in our willingness to trust in Jehovah's promises, to believe delivery will be made at a time chosen to give us the best results. The wonderful benefits that come as the result of positive powers will move your life forward. High risk roads will be replaced by the high powered roads you were meant to travel on. Isn't it wonderful to know that with just a small amount of the right kind of positive thinking, we can make our lives a whole lot better? Unannounced troubles will pop up every now and again. Even so, these unexpected problems do not have to push us into unfavorable lives. Depression is a bad season even for those who go in and out of it because it is so demanding of your attention. It drenches heavily as it robs you of peace and time. Your life can be bigger and better than the most positive thought you have ever allowed yourself. Your most brilliant positively powerful imagination can not begin to match Jehovah's plan for your future. Whatever the most powerful way is that you can imagine yourself being, you are billions of times more powerful than that. Our imagination cannot match God's. We could not have imagined ourselves, could we? We came alive through the blessings of a divine heavenly Power Source that is still with us today. Whether we acknowledge it or not, we were sent into the world with this blessed loving energy. You are many beautiful things yet to be discovered. Yes, you read that correctly. You are many beautiful things yet to be discovered. Because of the power and beauty placed within by the most blessed loving Hands, average is not a word that should ever be used to describe yourself. It's negative. Don't slap average on yourself. You were customized by the Maker of life. The Giver of life created nothing average. You are out of the ordinary.

You were not created for long-term success. Did I read that right?

Yes you did. You were not created for long-term success. You were created for infinite success. You were created by the One and Only original, professional Preparer. You were prepared for greatness. The mission to remove yourself from a life of sadness is not an impossible one. Faith and its positive filled energy can open doors no one can close. Make this your right time for restoration. Reject now each and every way you were taught to disappoint and abuse yourself. Give the most loving force a chance to direct your path. The dawning of your days should not be welcomed with a mind full of forced self-inflicted madness. The slavery of self-hatred is far worse than just an eroded way. It is acidic to human dignity. Our spoken positive intentions can be brought to pass. The sweet life that you are meant to enjoy should not be eaten up by a path of self-destruction. Dangerous thoughts can be erased from your thinking. Your most beautiful thoughts should always include the celebration of your one-of-a-kind life. Everyday of your life should be awareness day. Your life's victories should not be too few. Reassert your earthly authority back into your own life and know that you are still living in the hands of the ruling Power, a reign that will never end. You are not lifeless. You will never be totally alone. Keep faithing until you are comfortable enough to look up to the heavens and say, "I love this life show," and really mean it. Your own way of thinking should not work against you. No one should sit in the dark and cheer. Instead of wondering where the rest is, declare that you are blessed. Fulfill your remaining destiny using faith and courage. Yes you can. You can find courage in plenty. The Lord is still affectionately yours. Trust in the most High to reunite you with the courage denied you by sadness. You are the perfect combination of gifted power. You can be totally free from a life of mental misery. Seeing yourself as victorious will be a lot easier to do when your mind is focused the right way. We live in a world with an epidemic of human arrogance, ignorance and errors that can sometimes lift the innocent off their foundation, but once lessons have been learned and the educational value has sunk in, our human presence should not include a lethal harvest. You are the official result of the greatest Majority that there is. What that means is, you get to demand the largest share of happiness that is possible. You have a lot of leverage. Nothing born of devils should be allowed to grind you to a halt or even threaten your future. Claim your place up front. You know that you yourself are much more than a possibility. You are flesh and blood real. You are as real as it gets, so walk like it. Talk like it. Do your life as real as it was given to you. Walk with the kind of confidence the pressures of hell have never seen. Fear not. Do not be disturbed. Your life is already enveloped in greatness. The many blessings that can be found in the true faith are the sweetest, most everlasting relief that there is for the human soul. An overburdened soul is one being journeyed painfully incorrectly. Losing everything, mind first, was an incomprehensible thought that helped to change my bad habit of using the powers of my mind to revisit the places where the crimes were committed against me. Each time that I used the precious resources of my mind to take me back to these ugly, ungodly scenes, I would be left feeling as though I were being stabbed in the gut with a sharp iron anchor that went all the way down into my gut and then yanked me up off my knees and into the middle of a twister that always took way too long to pass. In that bad habit that I trained my mind to be in, there was not an ounce of true human freedom to be had. My life was on the most toxic of lines. My frequent visits back to the days that evil was applied to my innocence were certainly not a good way to live. That habit of looking back on and dwelling on the past, as you now know, almost destroyed me. I not only gave those toxic memories free reign, I also remained passive as they ripped through my soul and stole years from my life's time, a direct result of not knowing how to love and treasure my own humanity. I expected each day to be worse than the one before, and of course, they were. It took only a few negative remembrances to put the devil's wheels in motion. There was a breakdown at the very center of my soul. It was in this breakdown that I lost sight of the positive power in me. Jehovah created you as more living proof of His ability to perform miracles. Why not allow yourself to be the positive, powerful energy that you were created as? Were you to be blessed with the gift of one hundred and twenty years, it would still not change what was. Why waste a single day of your life? You cannot change what was, but you can certainly change for the better. The most quiet of times do not have to evoke the worst of memories. With the positive power of faith on your side, things will change in your favor. Many blessings are in store for you. Do not despair. Let your inner strength surface. It takes only a few steps of faith to lead you to the life you deserve. With faith in hand and heart, you can bloom anywhere. Being thankful for the small mercies will take you to the biggest mercies, proving once more the permanent link to the miracles that are so much a part of our make-up.

Think about the wonderful feelings of accomplishment and satisfaction that you get after you tidy up a room, or better yet, after someone else tidies it up for you. Tidying up your mind will give you the best freedom you have been denying yourself. Become an instrument of peace. You will be the first one to dance to its sweet miracles. Refuse to live in the confined space sadness has squeezed you into. Resist the urge to give up. Keep reminding yourself that you are a lovely creation of the Master, and celebrate your birth everyday. Your birth should not only be celebrated once a year. As human beings made from flesh and blood, we often get it wrong. The fact that you came into the world should be celebrated everyday in the most positive of ways. If you must blow your own mind, by all means, please do, but do it with kindness. It's the kind of rest your mind needs. If you decided to use your courage and determination, you can survive a whole lot better the things that often pull most people apart. Everything that you need for a rich new beginning is right there within your power. Use it. I don't know about you, but I am someone who is kept cheerful by the wonderful, natural, calming sounds of nature. Why not make a list of the things you love most about life, and then accept the permission that God gave you to enjoy them? You owe it to yourself to be happy. Perfect the art of you. Perfect the art of living. You can bring your life back as perfectly as God gave it to you. Don't give your mind to fear and torment. Reject the evil words of the wicked. Remove your life from the presence of those enemies who are working on your mind trying to convince you that you will never amount to anything in this world. Refuse to believe these ugly lies about you. Don't live with the devils lies. Refuse to let such lies become you. Bring your power out of its buried place, and then make the one and only Almighty proud. Only your most sincere effort is needed to get started. No one's life should be lived directed by someone else's insecurities. It should not still be going on. What does your life mean to you? Live to make you happy. There is noting wrong with being positively true to you. I am not suggesting total selfishness. What I am suggesting is that you pay closer attention to your own important needs. You cannot give your best to anyone if you can't even remember how to. Being luminous should not only be when you close your eyes. One of the important things I had to teach myself was how to daydream in beauty. I had to learn that living a great life had nothing to do with the material things still unattainable to most of us. The greatest joy that I have ever experienced is the miracle of living things. There are so many new insights that can be found in the great beauty of nature. It takes courage to triumph. One of these days should always be the one present, intelligent urgency will always be to your benefit. Your purpose is not to drink in the negative side effects of your fellow human beings. No one's negative energy should be allowed to override the positive power in you. Your journey is meant to be a journey of blessings. There is within faith a more secure ground made for your every step. You will be amazed by the breathtaking discoveries. You are one of the most important points that God has ever made. You were built with wisdom and maximum value. You have within you the right resources that you need to double up on your miracles. No antichrist has any power over you. Past mistakes, past abuses, recent mistakes, and recent mental and/or physical abuse should not be used as an excuse to continue punishing yourself. You should be defending your life against unpleasantness instead. Awareness and self motivation are among some of the nourishments that you need. You do not need more punishment. There are many wiser ways in which you can be more responsible for your own happiness, and you can do it inside and out quite nicely. If you are someone who has been living within the confinement of sadness for many years now, surely you must realize by now your life was not meant to be divided up, the biggest and most important share going to sadness. You are a reality to be cherished. You are a living, breathing fact. Don't ignore the fact. Take the time to discover those beautiful things about you yet to be discovered. There are millions of people living a life of discontentment, waiting for someone else to come along and make them happy, and until (if or when) that happens, they are willing to continue living a sad stagnant existence. That is such a foolish waste of precious mental energy. Living with such a mentality is definitely not a responsible strong way for anyone to live. If you are one who plans to wait for another person to come along and turn your life into a history of happiness for you, you are going to get very tired. Your happiness is also your responsibility. You can give to yourself many better tomorrows, effective immediately. Pay closer attention to your inner strength. You will be joyfully surprised. Defy the demons of depression and treat yourself gently. You are miracle's best match. You are one of God's greatest details. He will never fail to give you His attention. Hang in there. You are a child of the One and Only true Champion. Experience guaranteed! No one here on this earth can give you the benefit that the power behind the greatest Name can give you. You can have victory after victory after victory after victory. When it comes to toxic remembrances, you can avoid being transferred for lengthy periods of time. All of the violators must be avoided. The insecurities, the uneasiness, the ill treatments of self that began as the result of past disappointments are polluted leftovers that will continue to intensify your suffering. A healthy blend of positive thoughts is an automatic coming together of your better self. Your mind can be rescued from the darkness. There has never been a half moon, just hidden views of it. You do not have to live partly hidden behind dark clouds, regardless of whom or what convinced you to do so. You posses a blend of power that can outshine any darkness. Recovery and blessings is only your desire away. Desire to keep your connection to the wisest, limitless, ultimate Power Source. Start enjoying the beautiful heavenly classic that you are, instead of encouraging the bad reflections that will only continue to drain your brain's power. Those nasty clumps of disturbing memories do not deserve the opportunity to use your brain as a magnet. The hard fact is, too many of us humans enjoy being miserable. We invent new ways to self-destruct as often as we can. The human mind was not created to be polluted with horrors. If we were made to experience daily horrors, sadness would not be the cause of so many different types of health difficulties. Daily exposure to conflicts and other types of adversities has become highly addictive for some. The only barriers to the freedom of the positive human spirit are the ones we construct. Be determined to do whatever it takes to stay positive. Teach yourself how to blossom. Teach yourself something new everyday. Be that person that bakes the best bread in your town. Plant a vibrant flower garden of many different stunning colors, and then blossom right along with them. Everyday, choose a piece of clothing that matches the color of a flower. Continue doing so until you have gone through every vibrant stunning color of every flower. Then start over again, the second time around mixing the lovely combinations of colors. Be renewed like the flowers of Spring. There are countless beautiful things that you can do for yourself that will lift your spirits to new heights. Give to yourself lovingly. It is important to remember that you should be comfortable with your own life. To get comfortable with your own life, inner peace is a must. Sadness is not impossible to dismiss. Refuse to revert back to such thinking. Give your soul a chance at peaceful freedom. Allowing yourself to be used as a stomping ground for mental anguish is definitely not the way to use the generosity of life. It is time for you to give yourself a chance to experience life as the Maker intended for you to. For the rest of your life, everything that you do for yourself should be in comfort and healing. Your generosity should be channeled the right ways toward you. Carry in your mind, your heart and your soul that which will recharge you, not what will destroy you. You were not placed here to travel the journey in sorrow. Precious mental energy is being wasted when we become preoccupied with going into the dark depths that sadness demands that we do. Your life is too precious, too valuable, and too important to lose focus of it to internal hardship. You need to exercise your human right to live in the heart of peaceful energy. Don't lose faith, use faith. We are forever capable of more great things than we have ever taken the time to discover. Every good contribution that you can make to your own life is a step forward. The Almighty does reward our positive efforts. There is no limit to Jehovah's goodness. Give any reasonable request that you might have to the Almighty and believe for great things. Your faith will invite the very windows of heaven to open and pour out upon your life many blessings. Dream big. Dream beautifully day and night. Don't create nightmares in your head. Nightmares are the result of our troubled minds. Let your daydreams help to keep you healthy. Dream in faith.

The results of those prayers prayed will be your reality. The Lord is the best Accelerator you will ever trust. If such a positive power cannot accelerate your life, nothing else will. Perhaps you are so disillusioned with life at the moment that you don't believe you can feel better. You can feel better. Despite this turmoil filled world that we are sharing, you will feel better about life. Yes Jesus does love you too. Huge miracles continue to take place every moment of every day in every part of the world. You too can have your miracles. You do not have to suffer forever. Any reasonable intelligent person understands that being able to live a life of peace is the most basic of human rights. Don't give your rights away. Say, "No more will I surrender my precious days to emotional hardship." Say it, and mean it. You can change your life. You can be happy. Keep reminding yourself that every second of your life counts. Living sad is a gross misuse of one's life. I think it's safe to say that the majority of people in the world today do not want to see the rest of us sad. I believe it is also safe to add that those who flew on the wings of heavenly angels away from us too soon do not want to see any of us living a life of sadness. We will see them again soon enough. In the meantime, you have much to live for. Faithing is not risking. You have everything to gain. The ultimate sacrifice has already been made for your peace. It is up to you to benefit from the sacrifices that were made for our inner peace. Sadness is a misrepresentation of who we are as human beings. It would benefit all of us greatly if in the times we feel weak, we can remember to turn our problems over to the strongest Management that there is. Who else could you report your outage to and get maximum miracles? I believe very strongly in the renewal of the human spirit. Refresh your spirit everyday. A replenished spirit is a youthful spirit. In spite of the unbearable, you can still grow up in words of faith. What seemed so unbearable can become bearable. The unpleasant things that we are able to leave behind should be left right there in the past. Positive changes are very necessary if we are to move forward. The wise appreciation of life should never cease to be a directing force in our lives. Whatever the unpleasant news was that invited sadness, sadness itself is one of the worse news possible. Make the decision to be happy. You will discover the confidence to trust the Lord with all of your heart. The confusions and dark clouds will give way to brightness and newness. You will be so grateful for the restoration and the gift of time to meet the challenges you once feared. Faith as the positive power behind your thinking, as it does for me, will increase your survival. You can become an expert at enjoying your life. You can make a complete break from the things that left you feeling broken. Have full confidence in your ability to live your life without the abuse of spirit, body and soul. Adjusting to victory will be sweet.

Too many of our fellow human beings who suffered severe mental and physical abuse are spending valuable time envisioning disasters, unable to wrap their minds around peace simply because they have no idea how to. The peaceful nature that they were sent into the world with was taken away by abuse. Many have yet to experience the peace they desire. I have seen the best of humanity—we have all seen fellow human beings who cannot for the life of them envision themselves in the joyful realities they belong. Even though the idea of self-destruction did not originate with them, these fellow human beings developed a bad belief system that turned into a long running assumption of less importance. As a result, they end up handing their lives over to all other kinds of destruction beliefs, residing far from safety. What this should tell each and every one of us is that it is not wise to ignore one's own mental or physical discomforts. Unconditional love of self is such a precious gift, a gift too many of us refuse to give to ourselves. Instead we indulge in a daily ritual of self-condemnation. It makes no sense to keep ignoring one's own health, especially since we were given only one body. If you are unable or unwilling to love yourself unconditionally, who can you truly love unconditionally? Not loving yourself because you do not approve of the house of flesh in which your soul resides is unfair. No matter how you look at it, it is simply not fair. No one can ever have the best life possible while living with a mentality that included self-hatred. How can anyone who is determined to hate him or herself ever have the bright future that they should have? Positive thoughts are being brought into our reality everyday, but so are negative thoughts. If you allow a hateful, jealous person to convince you that you have no worth, that is exactly how the rest of society will see you, simply because we often times become our beliefs. We act out our secret thoughts without realizing how obvious they are to others. If you are feeling badly about yourself, a mind reader is not required for others to take notice of someone with a self-defeating mentality. Good or bad, the smallest of infants can feel our spirit. In this modern day world, the pressure to achieve material success is enormous. Is it any wonder then that depression has become such a wide spread problem for people of every age. A great many sufferers of depression did not fall into its grip because of a chemical imbalance in the brain. These unfortunate souls fell into depression forced by the belief that they had no other option but to give themselves over to be eroded. It is very tragic that so many people are living being plagued by the negative belief that they lack any kind of control over the direction of their lives. Children being the exception, it is certainly true that no child has the power and control over their own life, but the adult does. Obviously for those people who carried into adulthood that extreme negative feeling of, "I have no control over anything that takes place in my life so I might as well let life's unfairness toss me about like a leaf in the wind," is living a heart sick life, among other things. A negative mentality sends the wrong message every single time. Seeing yourself in a negative way can become an open invitation to all kinds of deviants. Like it or not, we live among some of the worst of users. When you show the world that you love and respect your own humanity, it sends a very clear message to any empty-headed bully whose intention it is to tear you down. Until you begin to see yourself as valuable as the Creator of life sees us, you will continue to make decisions that backslides your life. Allowing others to take over and control your most important life's decisions while you are still vibrant and able to do for yourself is not a healthy self-respecting way to live. Your life does not have to be tossed about by the barbaric, the selfish or by the envious. You can make the best decisions that are right for you. You can gather up your life's treasures and walk away from abuse forever. Yes you can. You can do it, and you can do it great. You can walk away and never look back. No longer should you be controlled by past or present criminal behavior. It is more than a little clear to most reasonable intelligent people that a lot of life's major frustrations could be avoided if we were all living with the positive healthy minds that were intended to provide us with the peace most of us desire. Of course, some of us are being driven to the brink of madness by fellow human beings that are horrible beyond comprehension. It is because of this unfortunate reality that so many people have given up believing that in spite of a world that included criminals, they can still find inner peace. This is especially true for those who have lost loved ones to murder. I too lost several family members to the insane criminal act of murder. In spite of this evil, I am determined to continue living the most positive peaceful life that I can. Whatever the reason or reasons for your sadness, living in sadness will not stop time from ticking away, nor will a heart sick with grief protect you from the passage of time. You cannot afford to forget that we have but one life. Please get on with yours. Love is available, more love than your heart can hold. Get back control of your life and start loving being alive. Refuse to become one of the unfortunate souls who stayed hooked on sadness to their last breath. Those were human beings who thought they had to suffer indefinitely in order to be human. There are billions of beautiful ways to be human. The Creator's given gift of freedom to us must be acknowledged and appreciated before it can be put to its best use. The freedom to live a happy life can not work for you in its positive powerful way until you accept and trust that the Almighty does not make mistakes. You cannot use for your benefit what you refuse to acknowledge. Depression is an enemy that can be defeated. There are many living proofs that it can be done. Take a commanding view of your own life. Let today be the day you realize you have suffered long enough. Spending the rest of your life being known by family, friends, coworkers, neighbors, and strangers as the unpleasant person who never smiles, does not make you inspiring to be around. A constant sad expression drags others down fast. Wouldn't it be wonderful if you became the person with the unforgettable positive presence, the one no one can resist, and the one whose presence everyone desires? Wouldn't that be great? Just imagine how fantastic a contribution you could make if you became that person whose very presence make others glad to be alive. You have much to offer this world. You can give to fellow human beings rich feelings of blessings with only a moment of your time. Help to enrich this world with love, hope, harmony, peace and grace. One of the spirits you lift will be your own. You can help to leave a lasting legacy of peace. You will not regret any positive changes that you make. Lots of wonderful things will continue to happen in your life. You cannot afford to give up. Keep fighting with faith. Fight despite the unnatural cruel ways that some people are determined to live their lives. Don't allow the bad behaviors of others to swallow up your entire life. Please don't waste another day of your life in a bad situation that you have the power to change. Give your lovely, loving self a more peaceful passage. Difficult emotional times need not be permanent for any survivor. You are a valuable worthwhile effort. Let your light shine through. Share a message of love, peace and happiness. I guarantee you your message of hope will be carried like a might wind circling the earth. You would be amazed how much beauty and joy a single heart felt smile can add to someone's day. You can be a source of calm and hope for many. As you read this, millions of people are dying for someone like yourself to care enough to lend them guidance, and you can. You can become wiser than sadness using the same spectacular, sustaining, restoring power that is responsible for every living miracle. The spiritual comforts that every soul need for a majestic life's journey is within your reach. Have faith that from now on, each day that you are blessed to behold will be better than the one before. Every morning that you wake up is a dream come true. It is a sin to force your minds to stay stuck on an unpleasant past. You can start living each day with a much better attitude. Start doing that. God promised you that you will prevail. Don't practice what you are not. You are not a loser. Most of us understand that life's difficulties can take many forms. Trouble comes in every size. The Almighty is bigger than all of them. In spite of any unpleasant forced changes, your value as a human being in the eyes of the Almighty remains the same. You still have the positive power to come up higher than you were before. You have within you the strength to resist the temptation to give up. Let putting up with negative thoughts be a thing of the past. I must remind you that your power comes in a twin pack, our Creator and you, a priceless bond that is not meant to be broken. You are power packed. You have the permission of the Divine to do all things good, which is another one of the reasons Jehovah never gives up on us. He has been waiting patiently for us to make peace on earth. If I am successful in getting this message of peace and love to your heart as well as to a permanent home in your mind, this will certainly be a day well spent for both of us. A single faith-filled prayer is more than enough to turn your entire life facing the right direction. Every human soul's journey is meant to be from glory to glory. It was not meant for you to waste a single moment of your time dealing with painful issues. It is true that we are all works in progress, but you can progress a lot better. With faith in heart, mind and soul, you can benefit from a limitless amount of progress. The low expectation of one's self that sometimes develops after years of sadness can keep you from your ambitions. In spite of any low opinions that you might have of yourself, you are still a whole human being. You are far more significant than the little attention you have been paid. God always has the right intention. The Almighty covered you in your mother's womb and is well aware of the problems you face today here on earth. There is no part of your life that is ever a secret to the Creator. All of our days were planned before we were even placed into the womb and none were meant to include a moment of evil's disruption. I am well aware that as wonderfully made as we are, human perfection is unreachable. Even so, there is endless perfection in the unconditional love that you can give to yourself. It is on of the most awesome gifts that you can give to yourself. When you care what happens to your own life, big gaps become rare and confidence is mighty. Living that way is the natural way to live. We are no ordinary creation. We came from the original winner which is why I am convinced we were not born to be losers. There is no broken spirit that cannot be made whole. We are made for great substance because we were made from great substance. See yourself as nothing less. Require of you the changes necessary for amore joyful life. Make the fact that you are so special to the Lord the main reason you accept being the winner you were born to be. When it comes to doing what is right for your own life, let no one turn you into a coward. One poor choice is sometimes all that is needed to risk a life time of the same. Living with a continued expectation of emotional pain will leave you with no shortage of criminals that will be more than willing to help you intensify it. Your life's journey should not be used for the abusive convenience of others. Now that you are no longer a child, refuse to make your life vulnerable to thieves. Give yourself the greatest life that you can. Most people who are blessed to be enjoying a great quality of life do not want a reduction in that fine quality of life. Be your own best influence. Give up living at the bottom of the toxic well mental hardship dragged you to. That is not a place you should become comfortable with. The other person who creates more awful disturbances in your journey should not be you. You should not be helping to throw your own life off track. Let no unfairness keep you tied to a lesser life. Your self worth should not be going in a different direction than you are going. A negative past should never ever be given your permission to rob you of the positive actions needed in the present. You are one of God's greatest insights. Not a single drop of your life was meant to be wasted. You were made with pure loving accuracy. You should be enjoying your life. Recognize your own inner strength. God is amazing. The power and the glory of God are still upon your life. You will be delivered. Faith is a fast heart and mind repairer only to name a few more of its brilliant gifts. Use this day as your day of new awakening. Make it no longer necessary for you to live on the brink of madness. Fight the negative influences with the most positive thoughts that you can imagine. The angels of the Lord will hear them. Your every request will be heard. You will receive from the most High supernatural miracles. You will never be out of God's favor. The maker of heaven and earth is still flowing strong. You need not suffer any further. Your long suffering can begin its ending today. You are able to make the necessary positive changes and be more in control of the out of control feelings. Those intrusive, painful remembrances do not own you. They do not have any right to lay claim to you. Refuse them. Don't let them confuse you. Embrace the security that comes with having a more peaceful life. Evolve in the delightful ways determined before your birth. No effort that you place in divine faith will ever be lost. The Almighty is not a hidden pathway. There is plenty of proof of that in every living thing. The Creator of the universe is a skillful transformer. Broken hearts are being mended everyday. You just have to have faith and trust that yours will be mended. You can survive adversity and be a lot stronger inside. Your many years of fresh, new, bigger, more powerful miracles are about to begin. Make up your mind to give the experience of God a try. Make up your mind to live in days of happiness. Demand your freedom back. Excel relentlessly. Be more determined to achieve the joyfulness approved by our Creator. Make room in your heart for blessings. Let heavenly blessings flow into your life from every corner of heaven. Tell God's angels you are ready to receive your blessings. Celebrate your existence. Celebrate the Inventor of the universe from Whom all blessings flow. There are countless ways in which you can contribute newness, peace, happiness, and most importantly, love to your own life. Denounce evil tongues and surround your life with people who live in deep unity, harmony and appreciation for the earth and its inhabitance. Live out the rest of your life in the presence of good influences. Use love to retrain your mind. A toxic past that is carried to the present is loaded with bad influences. Positive influences will help you to develop a greater understanding of your life's true purposes. You will get a brilliant insight into how incredibly special you are. You are a natural source for attracting miracles. You are blessed with the best ways of surviving beautifully in this world. It is right there within your own human power. Feelings of worthlessness and deep insecurities are the invention and work of the evil forces. Don't let these negative feelings spin you out of your rightful place. Don't give into them. Returning to the more peaceful free, soothing ways intended for our best survival is not and should not be difficult for any of us to accept. We cannot change for the better someone who is determined not to change. The victory is, we can change ourselves for the better. We can set ourselves free. We can free our minds of the tormenting invaders and move on ahead. We can be free to celebrate the rising of the sun each new day that we are blessed to have. Join into the Lord's good intention for your life. The steps forward will be many. Your great future is waiting and you can have it without the acid burns that went all the way through your soul. There is an endless supply of blessed assurance in the power of your faith. The rest of your days can be spent in the true spirit of fairness and newness. Be more dedicated to the evolution of self. The more wonderful you, full of greatness, is waiting to be free. Because our earth base is not for eternity is all the more reason why we should try harder to get as much of it right as we can. I know from first hand experience that not everyone requires steel bars to be imprisoned. I beg of you. Don't give up. Turn to the powers of sincere faith-filled prayers. Prayer changes things. Prayer can remove your mental anguish, not just ease it. The Lord is a best Friend of yours, the only best Friend that you can call on for help all the days of your life. My sincere prayer for you as I write this is for you to come to a place of peace in your life and be comforted a lot sooner than I was. Find that more intimate connection to the positive power within. Look forward to each new day with more gladness. Don't live your life angry. When we have enough faith to turn over to the Lord those who wronged us, the solutions are always ones we could not have thought of ourselves. Take it to the Lord in prayer. Staying active is good, but not in the art of self-destruction. Make your complaints directly to the one power that can change your life in profound ways. The search for the best you does not have to take you to a point of hopelessness. Things can go very smoothly if you are willing to let go of the old distorted view that you must live with an impoverish soul and be an emotional cripple. You already have in your possession the best technique for your rejuvenation that there is. You have the inner strength to reject fear and dangerous ignorance. You are not without the power to remove the hindrances hanging over from dark days. These nasty reruns should not be what bring you to your knees. Prayer should. Let the time for hellish reruns pass. You should not be passing the time with hellish reruns. Past unpleasantness should not continue to be disruptive to you no matter how disenchanted with life you have become. Must you life with an "I am only second rate" mentality? Must you? You cannot survive your best with the worst of mentality. Regardless of how hopeless things might seem to you, you are not without hope, condemning yourself to a life of inner conflicts is sure to interfere with the natural balance of your life. What you must also keep in mind is this. Sadness itself offers no solution to its root cause. A positive lifetime commitment to self is a much wiser choice. Seeking a better understanding of your own humanity will help lead you to your higher calling. There is no question about it. The unexpected cruelties that sometimes come with the human experience can be very discouraging. This I know all too well. Way back before I accepted fully that I am a part of something more significant than the constant echoes of hell that I lined up for me to welcome them everyday. I was sure that I had to accept this hell as the only way to live.

This ritualistic mental torture was what I had allowed myself to become accustomed to. As difficult as your experiences were, you can still give to yourself effectively an attitude of wellness. Think what a powerful gift that would be for you. The delicious power of positive thinking can fix a lot of things for you. It can reconstruct your life in ways that will remove you from the darkness permanently. The human body has its needs. That is something we can all agree on. What too many of us have lost focus of are the needs of the human soul. Our spiritual needs are just as important as the nourishment the human body requires to stay alive. The very earth upon which we walk gives us instructions and direction for a more peaceful way of life. The Lord is manifested in more ways than we are able to count or comprehend. Interestingly enough, what we do here on earth as we journey through really does matter, especially when it comes to how we care for ourselves and each other. I found out the hard way that prolonged sadness removes one's sense of place in the world. A beautiful transformation can be yours. You can become a much earthlier leader for your own life. A positive attitude is not only cleansing, but it will remind you of who you are, and who you came to this earth as. There is much more to your existence than meets your eyes. Real time cannot be bought. Make use of the free time that you are being given. Use it for your enjoyment. We have yet to find a way to replace a wasted or a well spent day. No sane person wants bad news, so why waste precious time on something that is of no good use to you? No remembrances that are less than beautiful and beneficial should parade through your life on a regular basis. Live with a brand new sense of "God always wins." That is more than enough of a reason to celebrate your life. You are going to wish you had started sooner. Protect yourself. You are a fortune, too valuable to hand over to depression. Please do not postpone living joyfully just so you can be preyed upon. You came into this world with a mind built for joy. Your very survival depends on you keeping it that way. It was intended for the world in which we live, to make more sense to us than it does today. Instead we live in a world where we encounter too many difficulties many of us are forced to go head-to-head with trouble everyday. There is no denying that truth, but those daily clashes that threaten to remove us from our sanity are not the original vision for us. Life's difficulties have pushed many over the edge. Sufferers of depression did not intend for this emotional difficulty to get out of hand and get stuck in mind with its serious health problems looming. It's a major headache that puts one in a most vulnerable position. If allowed to, it will most certainly pull you into a low life. Make no mistake about it. Depression is a major invasion, which is why some people need to also seek the help of a mental health professional. This is a positive step that I assure you will not offend God in any way. God is about the lives that He lovingly created. Do all of the positive things necessary for the revival that will place you upon the more solid foundation. You do not have to go it alone. The solid rock foundation you need is yours for the faithing. The fertile grounds for new, greater substance are already yours. The things that we allow to keep us in a state of constant sadness do not leave us enough room for the right kinds of growth. Sadness blights the human spirit and leaves us feeling we cannot get back the necessary control needed to harvest the positive power within. As we have all noticed, most weaknesses that we have are not good for us, whichever way you choose to look at it. Obviously, we cannot always leave in sad history what is sad history, but we can always allow ourselves enough peace of mind to become a solid overcomer. In the beginning, your life may not have landed in the best of human hands, yet this does not take away from the fact that you came from the holiest of loving Hands. No one here on this earth can make you less valuable to God, regardless of how run down you might feel. Don't live in fear of tomorrow. Put your trust in the most High. Let the wicked ones that walk among us be the ones to live with gut fear. You should not have to. Your time here is not to be spent embodying the tragic ideas of people whose daily ritual is their determination to deliver the devil's messages. Don't be poisoned by the belief that you are worth nothing. Don't ever believe it. Break that evil up. There is not one living thing that God created without value. The Almighty is very clear about that. I told that to you twice in this book because I don't want you to ever forget how truly precious you are. Accept that you too have every right to enjoy the benefits of a happy life. Be determined to go way beyond the low expectations of those who do not wish you well. Let those insecure, jealous people know that you will not be held back. Use the ultimate unconditional love as your guide. This is your time to emerge into newness. Don't let this opportunity pass you by. Being kind to yourself is pure success. I am not suggesting you toss discipline out of your life. Being kind to yourself does not have to be done in ways that will create new problems.

Your awareness in how you treat yourself is most important. The Almighty is watching over us, but there is no reason why you should not keep a wise eye on your own life. Too many of our fellow human beings lack the clarity one gets from having a sense of self. The sense of self that comes from the confidence in knowing one is loved. The sad sense that one is not loved has led to unintended, destructive behavior in way too many people. These deeply troubled fellow human beings fail to understand that they are love itself. It is what we were all created from, the same confident filled love that you too can use to your benefit. No more self-condemnation. This world was meant to be as happy as heaven is. As we can see, it is not always that way. Even so, you can make your own little heaven everyday right here on earth. Every time I find myself being challenged by unpleasant realities, instead of indulging in anger and bitterness, I remind myself that not every child who suffered the kinds of abuse I did survived to adulthood the way that I have been blessed to. You are still alive because your purpose has not yet been completed. Tormented souls can find peace. A time of anger can be changed into a time of blessings. I know from first hand experience how wonderful it is to have someone who loves you unconditionally and to whom you can tell your troubles and be assured your best interest is at heart despite your many angry complaints. What we cannot afford to ever forget is that the human kindness that we seek for ourselves must first be found in us. Inner peace and love of self will help us to look beyond any present problems that we may have. The unfairness we sometimes find ourselves suffering through should never be used as an excuse for self-hatred. One of the fastest ways to block your blessing is through self-hatred. Our thoughts do work on our lives in pretty much the same way that a sincere prayer does, even our most secret thoughts, which is why we must be careful of what we let loose in our mind. If you do not desire to have it, refuse to place it into your thoughts. Do not ask for it if you cannot afford to have it. If you are one who is convinced that you are an unlikable person that is a prophecy you are most likely to fulfill thousands of times over. On the other hand, if you live with the belief that you are the best that heaven had to offer to this earth, there are countless millions of fellow human beings who would love to be in the company of an earthly angel like yourself. Exercise continuously that which will enhance and lead you to more wonderful self discoveries. God is limitless in acts of love. Be limitless in your courage to do better for yourself. Try living that more peaceful life. Doing so will guarantee you a more enjoyable life. I am not suggesting you go off into the woods and become a bush baby. What I am suggesting to you, however, is that you give yourself the opportunity to live by the wise direction of the Divine, a direction that is already yours for the acknowledgement. Each breath that you take will be so much sweeter. Each day that passes will leave you more driven to love. Like so many children all over this world living in environments that include daily massive doses of human ignorance, my childhood story is also a very sad one, as you now know. What should have been the best time of my life became the worst time of my life. And if that were not enough, I have had to face challenges in my adulthood that were far more than I thought I could endure. Surviving them took faith on my part. It took guts, persistence, perseverance, and in spite of the fact that I sometimes believed I was born to suffer, I also had a strong relentless belief that I was born to do great things. From the time I was a small child, in spite of the mental and physical abuse I had to endure, I was not able to shake off the belief that I was created for a special purpose. The evil tongues were not able to lash this belief from my soul permanently, neither were the many beatings I suffered. Those assaults were no match for Jehovah's plans for me. Of course, because like you, I am only human, there were times since I've become an adult when I felt like giving up, but that strong feeling of special purpose deep down inside my soul always woke me up. Unfortunately, there still lies the possibility that for the rest of our lives from the time we might experience unfairness we just cannot comprehend or be forced to witness the unfairness applies to the lives of others. In spite of the evils in the world, I am now at a place of better understanding of how precious each new blessed day truly is. Every new day that we are blessed to have presents us with the chance to use the opportunity to change for the better those things that we can. Choose not to live in the narrow valley of depression, locked in its embrace of despair. Choose the power of faith and love to build you up from the ruins and place you high above it all. A life of full victory can be yours. Change your attitude to one that will allow you to appreciate how wonderful the gift of each new day is. It is possible to turn a painful past into a future of paradise. Choose to life out the rest of your life without a troubled heart. Be even more deeply honored to have been chosen to live in this new day. A good attitude about the gift of your life will keep you pressing forward instead of wasting precious time looking back on sour days. Enduring becomes a lot easier when we are willing to acknowledge the greater universal power that is always at work. No one gets away from the Almighty. Who among us can hide from the eyes of God? Hold your peace. God knows best how to fight our battles for us. He has seen your tears and has heard every prayer. Any kind of disruption in our mental or spiritual health is certainly not the will of God. Past or present difficulties should not keep overshadowing the rich value of you. Any toxic mental mess restricting your life should be replaced with the glorious, wonderful quality of life you were born to experience all the days of your life. At the present time, what you might be experiencing is the most difficult time of your life, which may not make it easy for you to believe that you are still in God's favor. You still exist on the love and mercy of the Almighty. You don't have to give up. Give into faith instead. Trust that you will make it through. This time too shall pass. You will be lifted out of trouble. Trust that all things are being worked together for good. Every one of us who chooses to be grateful for the opportunity to still be alive has the ability to inspire others. Use your God given inner strength to part company with sadness and worry. Don't worry, pray! Keep a special prayer in your heart always. Don't stop believing for new powerful miracles. Become a confident, towering, faith-filled presence that every devil will fear. You are a miracle. Wrap your mind around that instead. You have not seen anything in this world until you can see yourself as the beautiful, precious, special miracle that you are. You are remarkable. You are one of God's best. Love yourself just because you are. The Father of the universe did not put the spirit of fear in charge of you. Because of our own self doubt, we often fall victim to fear, even when it's unnecessary to do so. Living with the constant torment of fear and misery is very draining and as hurtful as landing on our head. Feeding fear and worry to our mind everyday will eventually knock the good sense out. Invite back into your life the heavenly peace you deserve. It is the right of every good, decent person to experience life as it was meant to be. If you continue to faith base your every breath, the clutters will be a lot easier to get through. It is possible to put an end to the feelings of emptiness and fear that sometimes take a hold of us. We don't have to spend every waking moment of our lives feeling disappointed. God leaves no room for doubt, we do. At the same time, we must bear in mind that not every disappointment equals failure. The best insights do not come from us. Ease the pressure. Let love, peace and happiness take over for a beautiful change. Faith in the awesome Power that rules the universe will keep you so beautiful you can look great, even at a hundred and eight. Be willing to eliminate the poisonous thoughts. Shut it off completely and start living a healing way of life. Trust that you can learn to live beautifully. The world still has so many beautiful things yet to be discovered by you. You are going to be so satisfied with the new opportunities a life of positive thinking has to offer. No more walls. No more barricades. You do not need to hide. You don't have to live traumatized. You are too precious to be entertaining cruel intrusive memories. Make it clear that you are no longer available to be trampled. Make it clear that you did not invite evil. Put hell back in its place. What defines you should not be a place in the torments of hell. Nightmares do not have to become you. You are better than that. Your placement here on earth was meant for you to be a beautiful light of peace among other positive contributions. You have an inner peaceful light that is so amazing in its beauty. If you so choose, it could be seen in you from miles away. Let your light shine strong. Let it shine through you like the heavenly beam that you are. Show heaven off. Let the rest of the world see what a piece of heaven looks like. You are a perfectly loved living soul. Let the idea of a very peaceful, soul-nurturing life become enticing to you. Run to a better way. Most of us can and should do a whole lot better with the time we are given. Be plentiful in joy. Contentment is a real find. There are more than just a few people in many parts of the world who wish they were able to live a more peaceful life, but are not able to do so because of fellow human beings in their environment determined to passage as selfish, consciousless, violent tyrants whose misguided beliefs include holding back time. Let's be honest. If you are someone who is free to experience a more successful life, to decide for yourself, to laugh as loud and for as long as you wish to, just to make a great big difference in your own life by living in a more meaningful way, yet still choose to remain unhappy, this should tell you that there needs to be a loving recommitment to self, one that includes whole purposes. Please don't misunderstand me. I am not saying that depression is an offense or that anytime spent on anything less than inspirational can not be forgiven. Of course, it can be forgiven. We live under the grace and mercy of the Almighty. It is how I know you can get it together using the same tiny mustard seed amount of faith that has been used to move mountains. You are wonderfully made. Press on, in spite of the offensive remembrances that will keep begging for your attention. Instead of living your life as a long-term pain recruiter, make this journey a remarkable one. Don't exit feeling incomplete.

www.ingramcontent.com/pod-product-compliance
Ingram Content Group UK Ltd.
Pitfield, Milton Keynes, MK11 3LW, UK
UKHW041944190726
13854UKWH00004B/1786